HAUNTED CLOSETS

TRUE TALES OF THE BOOGEYMAN

Katie Boyd

D1520144

4880 Lower Valley Road, Atglen, Pennsylvania 19310

Other Schiffer Books By Katie Boyd:
Rhode Island's Spooky Ghosts and Creepy Legends, 978-0-7643-3388-0, $14.99
Devils and Demonology In the 21st Century, 978-0-7643-3195-4, $14.99

Other Schiffer Books on Related Subjects:
Raising Indigo Kids, 978-0-7643-3391-0, $14.99
Ghost Quest in New Hampshire, 978-0-7643-2886-2, $14.95
Manchester Ghosts, 978-0-7643-2650-9, $14.95

Designed by "Sue"
Type set in Eraser/NewBskvll BT
ISBN: 978-0-7643-3474-0
Printed in China

Schiffer Books are available at special discounts for bulk purchases for sales promotions or premiums. Special editions, including personalized covers, corporate imprints, and excerpts can be created in large quantities for special needs. For more information contact the publisher:

Published by Schiffer Publishing Ltd., 4880 Lower Valley Road, Atglen, PA 19310
Phone: (610) 593-1777; Fax: (610) 593-2002 E-mail: Info@schifferbooks.com

For the largest selection of fine reference books on this and related subjects,
please visit our web site at: **www.schifferbooks.com**
We are always looking for people to write books on new and related subjects. If you have an idea for a book please contact us at the above address.

This book may be purchased from the publisher. Include $5.00 for shipping.
Please try your bookstore first. You may write for a free catalog.

In Europe, Schiffer books are distributed by
Bushwood Books
6 Marksbury Ave.
Kew Gardens
Surrey TW9 4JF England
Phone: 44 (0) 20 8392 8585; Fax: 44 (0) 20 8392 9876
E-mail: info@bushwoodbooks.co.uk
Website: www.bushwoodbooks.co.uk

DEDICATION

For all the victims of the Boogeyman who not only fought and lost, but also fought and survived.

ACKNOWLEDGMENTS

A special thanks to everyone at Schiffer Publishing, including Dinah Roseberry...you're the best...and Peter Schiffer for having such wonderful faith in my work...you are awesome! A great big special thank you goes to Jennifer Marie Savage, my editor, for her patience and hard work. I very much appreciate the dedication you have given to this book!

Thanks also to Beckah Boyd, for always keeping me on track with my writing and believing in me!

CONTENTS

INTRODUCTION

It all started to go downhill for my family when I was five years old — that is when I had my first experience with the legendary creature we call the boogeyman. It was not a movie or a story, but an actual encounter...one that would last for years to come. My father had gotten a promotion at the telephone company he worked for, causing the family to have to pack up and move to New Hampshire from Massachusetts. I was two years old at the time.

We bought a quaint yellow house in Goffstown, New Hampshire, a quiet area that my parents believed to be good for raising kids, and over the first couple of years, my grandfather and father renovated the whole house from top to bottom — the entire footprint of the house was changed. The first bedroom I stayed in was small; I remember my mother used to put up a security gate in the doorway of my room. I used to stand behind that gate and hold on watching my mother cleaning or doing chores upstairs. I was so comfortable in the small room that I actually used to hang out on one of the low shelves inside the closet. However, as I got older, my parents decided to move me into my brother's room. I was getting bigger, so my mother decided I needed a bigger room. I soon discovered that I was not the only one who resided in my brother's room.

Before I moved into the room, I used to play with my brother there. That was my first encounter with "Fire Face." We will save that story for later in the book. I never really hung out in my

Here I am with my brother in Acton, Massachusetts, before our move to New Hampshire.

bedroom, even during the day. At first, it seemed as though I was unwanted by this presence. Over time that changed and soon I was spending all hours in my room. The more time I spent in the room, the worse the activity would get.

Every time I would go into my room to settle down for bed, the closet door would open. I would ask my mother when she came in to close the closet door. She would, and then she would tell me goodnight and leave. Mind you, my bed was directly across from the closet I so feared. Every night the nightmares came, every night the closet door opened...and an unsettling presence would slowly approach my bed. Hours would pass between the time of going to bed and hearing the closet door open during the night. Like most parents, mine did not believe my stories of the monster that lived in my closet and came out at night. As each of us grows up, it seems we forget about our childhood fears and experiences. I have not forgotten...ever.

We watch movies with all types of paranormal themes or movies with fake monsters that come out at night and try to get us. Could the monsters in the movies be a reflection of the real boogeyman? Alternatively, could it be a reminder that even as an adult, our childhood fears are still dwelling inside us?

Follow my own experiences with the boogeyman throughout this book and read about the real cases of victims who have dealt with this sinister entity. Discover the phenomena known as sleep paralysis, find out where nightmares really come from, and discover that dark place where reality and dreams collide to create a frightening picture in a person's mind. Read both ancient and modern boogeyman legends from around the world. Learn the telltale signs between a nightmare and a visit from the real boogeyman. Explore the world of real serial killers dating back from the 1800s and read how some flesh and bone men have perpetuated the boogeyman myth. Learn the full stories behind our favorite fictional horror characters that we just love being scared by. Read firsthand accounts of families being terrorized by the unknown, and find out what happens when I am personally called in to help.

So come join me on this venture into a world that is not our own... but the *Boogeyman's*.

Section One:

WHO IS THE BOOGEYMAN?

Chapter One:
BOOGEYMAN MYTHS AND LEGENDS

> "Hush little baby, don't say a word
> And never mind that noise you heard
> It's just the beast under your bed,
> In your closet, in your head."
> ~ Sandman, by Metallica

Almost every culture has some form of the boogeyman. In fact, there are over seventy names for this horrible creature that kidnaps and preys on young children! Whether it's Iran, Canada, England, Scotland, Wales, Ireland, or the United States of America, each culture has its own version, but they all include the same modus operandi: if the child does not behave, then that child is fair game for the boogeyman. Because the boogeyman is present in every culture, psychologists believe that the boogeyman myth and others like it stem from an evolutionary throwback to prevent children from wandering from a tribal homestead or group in order to better protect them from predators. Wherever you travel, even in the United States, the boogeyman myth changes; to some it is a man, to others a woman. In some areas, they believe the boogeyman appears as a green fog, and in the Midwestern states, they do not believe that the boogeyman enters the house or bedroom, but rather he scratches on the window.

Regardless, though, of individual beliefs about this creature, a central question remains: Where does the boogeyman come from? Well, most etymologists believe that it comes from the Middle English word bugge or bogge, which has ties to the Scottish "bogle this" creature and is one of the faery-folk; however, not every faery is pretty and kind. Oh, no, a bogle is a bad character with a fierce temper. They love to drive humans insane with their trickery, such as calling of names (for instance it calls your name in the hallway, but when you peek out your bedroom door, no one is there) and stealing objects (your wallet is there one minute, the next it's upstairs in your bedroom), but this does not occur simply once or twice. No, a bogle will not stop until they feel you are quite out of your mind.

I have categorized this chapter into two separate sections; the first is all about the Bag Men. These are the boogeymen that snatch kids off the streets or out of their homes, throw them in a sack, and take them away to eat. The second is far more nefarious. At least with the first, if you see a person running after you with a giant sack, you know what is coming next; with the second type, you will never see it coming. These are the monsters under the bed. The nightmarish fairytale figure comes to life to eat the flesh and bone of a misbehaving child. I said it before in my book *Devils and Demonology in the 21st Century* and I will say it again: What you can see in this world could hurt you, but what you cannot could kill you.

THE BAG MEN

There are so many myths and legends surrounding this mysterious being from Irish folktales to almost comical miscommunication between languages. Take Quebec's own boogeyman, the Bonhomme Sept-Heures, or the 7 o'clock man, for example. This character is a traveling peddler who carries a large burlap sack with him and wears a long overcoat where the pockets are deep enough to hold children. His favorite hiding place is under the porch and he prowls the streets after 7 o'clock looking for kids who did not get home on time or stayed up past their bedtime. He scoops as many kids up as he can and then moves on to the next town. The fascinating thing about the Bonhomme is not so much his nature, but his name. It is a fabulous example of an English word being misunderstood and mispronounced by a French-speaking society with little knowledge of the English language. Say the word "Bonhomme Sept-Heures" to yourself and you can hear an attempt at saying "bonesetter."

It is not surprising that they would turn a worker in this profession into a boogeyman. Many of the citizens of Quebec at the time did not have access to doctors or nurses and so the patient would wait for the bonesetters to come. Both men and women alike practiced the art, but, unfortunately, around this time there was no such thing as a local anesthetic and the whole village would hear the screams of the patient. Part of the mythology that surrounds the Bonhomme Sept-Heures is that he would take children as payment for his services to a family.

The French are particularly interesting. The boogeyman of these children's nightmares is called Le Père Fouettard or, when translated, Father Flogger, the not so nice version of Father Christmas. He has even once or twice stolen the jolly man's identity! Father Flogger's name has been linked to Santa Clause since the fourth century. Here is a seventeenth century children's song about how St. Nicholas met Father Flogger. It truly is a morbid story... and typical of the times.

Original French

Il était trois petits enfants,
Qui s'en allaient glaner aux
  champs.
Ils sont tant allés et venus
Que le soleil on n'a plus vu.

S'en sont allés chez un boucher,
"Boucher, voudrais-tu nous
  loger?"
— "Allez, allez, mes beaux
  enfants,
Nous avons trop d'empêche-
ment."

Sa femme, qu'était derrière lui,
Bien vitement le conseillit,
"Ils ont, dit-elle, de l'argent,
Nous en serons riches
  marchands."

Entrez, entrez, mes beaux
  enfants!
Y a de la place assurément.
Nous vous ferons fort bien
  souper,
Aussi bien blanchement coucher."

Ils n'étaient pas sitôt entrés,
Que le boucher les a tués,
Les a coupés tout par morceaux,
Mis au saloir comme pourceaux.

Quand ce fut au bout de sept ans,
Saint Nicolas vint dans ce champ.
Il s'en alla chez le boucher,
"Boucher, voudrais-tu me loger?"

English Translation

Three little children they were,
In the fields three little gleaners.
They gleaned and gleaned
Until the sun disappeared.

They knocked at the door of a
  butcher.
"Butcher, will you give us shelter?"
"Not here, my little darlings,
We offer no lodging."

His wife, standing behind him,
Slyly whispered in his ear,
"They have," she said, "gold and
  silver.
You will become a rich merchant."

"Do come in, my little darlings,
For sure you can have lodgings.
You can have a good supper,
And sleep under a warm cover."

No sooner did they enter, then
They were slaughtered by the
  butcher,
Who cut them up and threw their
  parts
Into a salting tub, just as pork
  pieces.

Seven long years had passed,
When St. Nicholas visited here.
As he was tired, he went to the
  butcher,
"Butcher, would you have shelter?"

Original French

"Entrez, entrez, Saint Nicolas!
De la place, il n'en manque pas."
Il n'était pas sitôt entrç,
Qu'il a demandé à souper.

"Voul'ous un morceau de
jambon?"
— "Je n'en veux pas, il n'est pas
bon."
— "Voulez-vous un morceau de
veau?"
— "Je n'en veux pas, il n'est pas
beau."

"De ce salé je veux avoir,
Qu'y a sept ans qu'est dans le
saloir."
Quand le boucher entendit ça,
Hors de sa porte il s'enfuya.

"Boucher, boucher, ne t'enfuis
pas!
Repens-toi, Dieu te pardonn'ra."
Saint Nicolas posa trois doigts
Dessus le bord de ce saloir.

Le premier dit, "J'ai bien dormi!"
Le second dit, "Et moi aussi!"
A ajouté le plus petit,
"Je croyais être en paradis!"

English Translation

"Pray, come in, Saint Nicholas,
I will not leave a holy man
homeless."
No sooner did he enter,
When he asked for some supper.

"D'you want a slice of ham?"
"I won't eat ham, no matter how
hungry
I am."
"D'you want a nice piece of veal?"
"I do not want, it is not real."

"How about salted meat in this tub?
This I would gladly eat."
As the butcher heard the Saint
speaking,
He took to his heels, to run afar.

"Butcher, butcher, don't try to flee—
Repent and God will forgive thee."
Then, Saint Nicholas placed fingers
three
On the rim of the salting tub.

The first child said, "I had a good
sleep!"
The second said, "Mine was so
deep!"
The youngest one opened his eyes,
"I thought I was in Paradise!"

~ Translated by Daniel Police,
La Flèche, France

Le Père Fouettard

Le Père Fouettard was also known as "Father Flogger." *Courtesy of billcasselman.com.*

The seven years that the song alluded to is actually the time after St. Nicholas' death. The butcher, knowing that the holy man had died prior, figured out quickly what the saint was after. Old St. Nick gained a reputation as a protector of children. For the butcher's punishment, he was cursed to become Père Fouettard; he dresses in a black robe and stuffs bad children into a big black sack that he carries over his shoulder and hits them with a stick or whip. Some legends say he is condemned to walk behind Father Christmas and to accept the shame, and angry words that people hurl at him while the holy man makes his rounds. Still others say that he merely follows St. Nicholas, not as a servant or as a condemned man, but more like an apostle in thanks to the saint for saving his soul.

Spain's Bag Man

Brazil and Portugal have their own boogeyman in the form of the El Hombre Del Saco, aka "The Bag Man."

Spain has also adopted this nefarious figure and, much like the other myths, the tale is simple: If a child is out late at night, does not eat all of their food, or does not go to bed on time, then they will be snatched by the Bag Man and taken away forever. He appears as a frail old man, both mean and ugly, and is mostly found haunting alleyways and dark corners waiting to reach out and grab a child to throw in his bag. Again, this sounds very much like all of the other boogeyman myths you have read so far. However, this one has some factual base to it.

Back in the sixteenth and seventeenth centuries, there were quite a few of these Bag Men. They were charged with the task of gathering orphans found on the streets to bring to a local orphanage. Yes, they were doing good work; however, the method was both crude and torturous for the child. He would dump them into a huge bag or wicker basket and walk the town, city, or even the entire province looking for more. It was about quantity not quality and many of the children died before they even made it to the orphanage because of lack of care and the unhealthy mode of transport.

Haiti's Bagman

In Haiti, it is not so much a matter of myth taken from reality, but a horribly terrifying myth that seemed to be brought to reality. The boogeyman of Haiti is called Tonton Macoute or Uncle Gunnysack. Much like in French folklore, from which many Haitian Creole draw their modern mythical icons, Uncle Gunnysack is a counterpart of Father Christmas; the only difference is that he was not a butcher, but rather a giant. However, he, like all of the others, carried a sack to throw misbehaving children into.

In 1957, François Duvalier, better known as Papa Doc, came into power; he was democratically voted into office after serving as Minister of Health for a number of years. In 1959, Papa Doc formed the National Security Volunteers. These people reported directly to Duvalier and those who spoke out against Duvalier risked being abducted themselves; if anyone ever challenged Papa Doc's authority or that of the NSV, they would fade away as if they never existed, carried off into the night. Therefore, to further the boogeyman myth in Haiti, they began to call themselves Tonton Macoute because they did with adults what Tonton did with children — snatched them and made them disappear forever.

FAIRYTALE FIGURES AND MAGICAL BEINGS

Baba Yaga

A prominent figure in Russian folklore, Baba Yaga is the infamous witch that flies about on a mortar using the pestle as a rudder and a broom made of silver birch to cover her tracks. Her name, which literally translates to "Bony Leg," fits her physicality; she is a thin and bony old woman with iron teeth. She loves the taste of children and often kidnaps them, presumably bringing them back to her home to eat. She has an insatiable appetite, but can never gain an ounce of weight. Almost like a hungry spirit, she is never quite full and is always on the hunt for more children.

Baba Yaga rides on her mortar and pestle back home to her cottage on chicken legs after snatching a child. *By Viktor Vasnetsov, circa 1917. Courtesy of Wikipedia.*

It is said that Baba Yaga lives deep in the woods in a hut that sits on chickens' feet. It is constantly revolving and, as it does, it releases a bloodcurdling scream. Baba Yaga takes this protective measure so no one can get in or out when she is not home. The only way to stop the home from spinning is a secret incantation. When the words are spoken, the house will stop spinning and the chicken legs will lower the building to the ground, and the door will crash open on its own to allow the person entry. The home is often depicted as having a wall of skulls with three pikes; two with skulls on them. The other lays empty waiting for the hero/heroine or victim. Every once in a while someone will make it to her home; if Baba Yaga is home, she will ask whether the individual comes of their free will or if they were sent. There is only one right answer, so pray if you ever come upon her, you know it.

Baba Yaga is not friendless. She has three "soul friends" that mysteriously appear as pairs of hands to give her whatever she may require in her home. Baba Yaga also has control over the elements and three other servants who reside outside of her home. They are the three horsemen: white, red, and black knights. The White Knight will shoot an arrow into the sky causing daybreak; Baba Yaga calls him "my bright dawn." The Red Knight will shoot an arrow into the sky causing the sun to rise; Baba Yaga refers to him as "my red sun." Finally, the Black Knight brings the night when he gallops up; the witch refers to him as "my dark knight."

Baba Yaga has gotten around within Slavic culture. In Poland, she is known as "Baba Jaga," and, in Czech and Slovak, "Ježibaba." In Slovene, the words are reversed, producing Jaga Baba. Bulgarian uses Баба Яга; and Ukrainian, Баба Яга. When translated, the last two also mean Baba Yaga.

However, in Southern Slavic traditions, the Baba Yaga entity exists under a slightly different name: Baba Roga, in Croatia and Bosnia, and a similar Baba Posa in Macedonian/Serbian. Roga literally means horns or horned. Therefore, it would be "old horned woman." It does not matter what you call her, though — all that matters is that you remember this: if you see a house on chicken legs spinning in the middle of the forest walk the other way… QUICKLY.

Bicho Papão

An even better boogeyman from Brazil is the Bicho Papão. Many a mother has said to her child:

"Minha filha, quando você for dormir, corra para cima da cama e lá permaneça a noite toda! E nunca olhe para baixo, senão o bicho papão vai te pegar!"

~~~~~

Translation: "My daughter, when you are going to sleep, run up to the bed and there remain all the night! And never look down; otherwise the boogeyman is going to catch you!"

Many a child did just that — hid beneath the covers for fear of this particular boogeyman. The Bicho Papão or "The Eating Beast" actually maintains nocturnal habits; he sleeps during the day and rises only at night when his prey is sleeping, nestled under their covers. It only goes after children who disobey their parents or do not eat in a manner to their parents' satisfaction. This character was originally taken from the folklore of the Portuguese and instituted as a full-fledged monster in Brazil, although there is no confirmation as to what it was. It's considered a man-animal type figure.

El Cuco

Let us not forget the El Cuco or El Coco. There are feminine versions of this character, but they are indistinguishable from their male counterparts. This figure has traveled all over the Hispanic community. Now if you go up to a Spanish or Portuguese speaking person today and you ask them if they have seen the El Coco, they may think you are asking about their head, a pumpkin, or a coconut! The reason for this is that in 1498 when Vasco Da Gama and his crew discovered the coconut with its three holes that looked like hollow eyes and a mouth and its hair skin it reminded them of the fearsome El Coco. The word Coco first appeared in 1445, written in the Canionero by Antón de Montoro. He says:

Original Spanish	English Translation
tanto me dieron de poco	I was so little
que de puro miedo temo,	of that pure fear I am afraid,
como los niños de cuna	as the children of cradle
que les dicen ¡cata el coco!	that say to them: look at the coconut! ....

Here is a more modern version done to the tune of Rock-A-Bye Baby:

Duérmete mi niño, duérmete ya...
(Sleep my child, sleep now...)
Por que viene el coco y te comerá.
(Or else the coco will come and eat you.)

"Que Viente El Coco," circa 1799. *Courtesy of Wikipedia.*

The El Cuco, which actually means "cuckoo" and not coconut, has so many different names across the Spanish and Portuguese speaking community that it is hard to keep up.

† In Peru, he is called Cucufo, which is one of the names of the Devil himself.

† In Cuba, you will often hear him called the name Cocoricamo.

† In Mexico, there is the Kukui.

† In the United States, this creature is typically called Cocoma.

There are several different descriptions of this entity; some say it looks like a wolf that stands upright on two legs, holding a flogger with which to beat bad children. Others say it looks like an egg with two sticks for arms and two for legs and large eyes. Yet others still claim that El Coco is a human child spirit that died due to violence and often appears as a quasi humanoid with glowing red eyes. Either way, many a mother has threatened their children with the El Cuco since at least the fifteenth century! They are a type of entity that must be invoked in order for their wrath to be unleashed upon misbehaving youngsters.

Namahage

Most parents never expect to meet the boogeyman, let alone have to negotiate with them for the life of their child. Well, in Northern Japan they do. In the ancient mountains of the Oga Peninsula live the Namahage, an old race of demons that come down every New Year's Eve to collect misbehaving children and skin them. Figuratively speaking, Nama actually refers to the patch of skin that develops when you sit in front of the fire too long, and Hage means scrape or "to scrape."

No one knows exactly when the Namahage myth began, but the townspeople continue the centuries' old tradition to this day. There are many theories as to where they originally came from; one is that they were mountain deities. Japanese mythology, much like the Greeks, had a lot of God and human interaction where the Gods would come and mingle, harass, or bless the humans. However, the Gods did not come down in a giant parade like the Namahage do every year. Yet another theory is that the Namahage were in fact shipwrecked European explorers like the Vikings.

Nevertheless, the Namahage is an intimidating character and the legend behind them is just as frightening. The old stories say that the Namahage came and were making a lot of trouble for the people of Oga, so the people decided to make a deal with the demons. Thinking that they would not win the bet, the townspeople that if the Namahage could build a 1,000-step staircase to the main shrine before morning, the townspeople would give them one girl a year. If they failed, they were to leave the town alone. The Namahage, who revered hard work and scorned laziness, worked deep into the night tirelessly. As the villagers watched, their faces fell in horror; dawn had not yet broken — in fact it was still hours away — and the Namahage only had one stone step left to put in place! One of the townsfolk was incredibly bright and decided to crow like a rooster. The Namahage, thinking they had lost the bet, returned to their mysterious mountain home.

However, they come down every year — only at night — waving torches and large butcher knives, dressed in straw robes. Namahage are both male (they have a red face) and female (they have a blue one) and are loud; they howl and stomp, letting everyone know of their presence. The Namahage parade through the village in search of lazy children (I guess in compensation for building 999 stairs), banging on the doors of homes where parents await their arrival.

The Namahage storm into the house, stomping and howling, in an attempt to grab the children and scare them. They will ask the parents if they have any lazy kids. If they do, you had better watch out...for the Namahage loathe laziness and tears above all else. It is said that if they find an indolent child, they will skin them and eat them or bring them back up to the mountain to use as slave labor. The parents will have Saki and a special meal prepared to placate these evil beings. While the demons eat and drink their fill, they open a special book they keep that has a list

A male Namahage. *Courtesy of Masa.*

of the children's names and offenses. The parents inform them that there are no idle children, nor will there be for next year. They also use this time to ask for blessings on the home and crops. If the Namahage are appeased, then they will bestow their blessings while stomping and howling over to the next house. For the rest of New Year's Eve, the Namahage travel from home to home, scaring children into obeying their parents and instilling a fear of slothful behavior.

It is a glorious affair. If you can ever go to see a procession of the Namahage, I suggest you do. The younger children cry their eyes out at the frightful appearance of these entities while the older ones attempt to grab a piece of their straw robe. If you can get one, it is considered to be of great luck. At the end of the festival, the Shinto priest presents an offering of mochi (a rice cake burned black by an open flame) that the Namahage begrudgingly accept as they head back up the mountain. The Namahage never go away... they wait, watching and making a list so that they will be prepared for next New Year's Eve.

Rawhead and Bloody Bones

An Irish boogeyman figure, Rawhead and Bloody Bones, goes by a few different names, such as Old Bloody Bones and Tommy Rawhead. It is a truly dark and twisted myth that has evolved over time. Although the legend originated in Ireland, it has spread to the rest of the United Kingdom, particularly Midwest and Southern America.

Bloody Bones

Originally, it was believed that Bloody Bones could be found near water, especially old marl–pits or deep ponds. He would reward good children and punish the bad by drowning them. However, modern amenities have made the access Bloody Bones has to children much easier. He is now known for living beneath the sink, specifically in drainpipes. In addition, he has one of the most potentially frightening abilities imaginable: he can turn naughty children into some inconsequential form — like a piece of paper — that would literally cause the parents to throw their children away. There is a short, one stanza poem that originated in Yorkshire/Lancaster about this particular boogeyman:

> "Rawhead and Bloody Bones
> Steals naughty children from their homes,
> Takes them to his dirty den,
> And they are never seen again."

Rawhead

The appearance of this boogeyman is highly debated depending on where you go. Some say he is just a skeleton; others say he looks like a giant decaying boar or pig. Georgess McHargue talked about one of the oldest and most common descriptions in her book The Impossible People, where she said Rawhead "is rumored to have a crouching form like a rock. He is covered all over with matted hair, has pale flat eyes, and lives in dark cupboards." In other descriptions, he is much like the ever-feared Irish Pooka that many believe can change form at will.

Early on Rawhead was mixed into our culture. The first mention of him is in the fifteenth century when Rawhead and Bloody Bones lent his name to us for our pirate flags of the skull and crossbones! He has also made appearances in modern folklore; he's been in comics, books, and television, playing both major and minor roles. As we continue to acknowledge and honor his existence, I have to think that maybe Old Bloody Bones is sitting in a drainpipe somewhere, cackling with laughter over our lackadaisical attitude toward ancient mythology and folklore, as he gets ready to drag another child down the pipe.

Chapter Two:
THE PARASOMNIA PHENOMENON

> "Do you know the terror of he who falls asleep?
> To the very toes he is terrified,
> Because the ground gives way under him,
> And the dream begins..."
> ~ Friedrich Nietzsche

Parasomnia, which means "around sleep," is an umbrella term for a whole host of sleep disorders that can cause abnormal or unnatural movement, dreams, behavior, and perception. It is more common to find these conditions in children rather than adults, although it does happen. The different kinds of parasomnias include narcolepsy, night terrors, sleep paralysis, and hypnagogic hallucinations, which are covered further on in this chapter.

Sleep disorders can cause a whole bunch of issues; insomnia is only one of them and it causes you to wake up and feel even more tired than you were when you went to bed. Nightmares are not a part of parasomnia, but they are a sleep disorder all the same. Although nightmares are usually considered a bad or scary dream, which may cause emotional and unpleasant responses such as fear, anger, guilt, or a feeling of anxiousness. With nightmares, there are sometimes strong sensations of pain or sensations of action, such as falling or being chased by an unknown person or image. Many doctors today believe nightmares to be caused by high fevers, psychological trauma, stress, traumatic situations, and eating heavily before going to sleep. Some ways to subside the nightmares would be trying meditation, yoga, exercising, and eating more healthy foods.

NIGHT TERRORS AND NIGHTMARES

Night terrors are also known as Pavor Nocturnus — when literally translated, it means "panic at night" or "fear at night." It's a state of extreme terror in which the individual is temporary unable to gain full consciousness. This is not the same as a nightmare. In many cases of night terrors, an individual abruptly wakes up; usually their eyes are open, but even though they may seem fully awake the victim is not completely conscious, and suddenly are gasping for air, moaning, or even screaming. At this point, it is impossible to wake the victim from the night terror — and the sleeper does not normally remember the episodes of these events. Night terrors can last from ten minutes to a full half hour. Some researchers claim that night terrors are caused by some form of a "misfire" in our brains and can be caused by stress or a medical ailment. There are several differences between nightmares and night terrors:

Nightmare: Occurs in REM sleep (approximately 90 minutes afterfalling asleep)
Night Terror: Occurs in non-REM sleep (about an hour after falling asleep)

Nightmare: Wakes up with a vivid memory of the dream
Night Terror: No recollection of the event or dream

Nightmare: Scares the victim (child or adult)
Night Terror: Scares the caregiver or friend

Nightmare: When they "wake up," they will be aware of their surroundings.
Night Terror: It seems they wake up, but in fact are not and will not recognize their surroundings or familiar voices and faces.

Nightmare: Needs to be comforted... Who doesn't want hugs after a bad dream?
Night Terror: Cannot be comforted... Since they cannot recall the episode, they typically go right back to sleep.

Nightmare: May complain about insomnia
Night Terror: Never complains about lack of sleep, but of odd movements or waking up in a different area or in an odd position.

These are some of the biggest clues we have to differentiate between a nightmare and night terror. Once you have an idea of what it may be, it is generally easy to get a full diagnosis by spending some time in a sleep lab or talking extensively with your doctor. If you do spend time in a sleep lab, you will most likely come to know a wonderful tool called the Polysomnogram. It records the sleep stages that a patient goes through as well as the respiratory events that occur during sleep. Night terrors do occur in adults, but is actually experienced most commonly by pre-adolescent boys. Let us take a closer look at the effect night terrors and nightmares have on both children and adults.

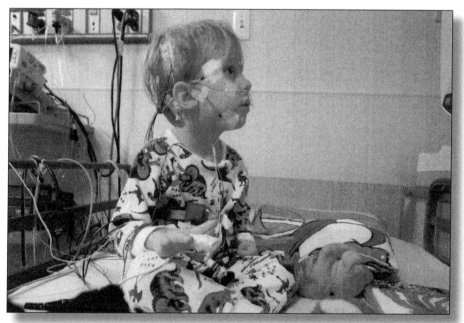

A pediatric patient is being prepped for a polysomnogram at St. Louis Children's Hospital in St. Louis, Missouri. *Courtesy of Robert Lawton, 2006.*

The Children's Experience

Night Terrors

Affecting fifteen percent of all children — and three percent of the total population — night terrors are frightening and can be as traumatic for the parent as they are for the child. Studies have shown that night terrors do run in families, and pre-adolescent boys are typical victims, but inquiries into this frightening sleep disorder have found that children suffering from this affliction are most commonly between the ages of three and twelve years of age.

One of the biggest things you can do to help a child overcome their night terrors is to establish a routine. Make extra time to do some activities that will help them relax before bedtime, such as reading or taking a bubble bath. It is best if the child can have their own room to minimize disturbances. However, if you have two boys and they sleep in the same room, what you can do is put them to bed about an hour or hour and a half apart, so that the distractions and conversations that would typically occur cannot. This leads to an easier sleeping experience. Most children's night terrors can actually be caused by lack of sleep; this is why establishing a routine is so important.

Night terrors in children typically occur between fifteen minutes to an hour after the child has fallen asleep. If you notice your child is having the episodes consistently and at around the same time, as a means of prevention you could wake them up a few minutes before. This is almost like causing their brain to reset. If you think of the brain like the gears on a car, where typically your child's brain would shift into overdrive, by waking them up you are putting them essentially in neutral so the rest of the night they can coast along in golden dreams.

Nightmares

To a child, nightmares are a very frightening, very real experience and most parents usually will calm the child down with by talking to or hugging the child. After the child is calmed down, the parent sends the child back to bed for the rest of the night. As soon as the parent leaves the child's bedroom, the child is hiding under the bedcovers and praying that no monsters will come for them.

I was very young, around six or seven years old, when my nightmares started. Every night at midnight my nightmares would wake me in such a horrific state of mind. I would find myself running down the dark hallway heading for my parents' bedroom for safety. There was always a feeling of protection once my feet hit their bedroom floor. Curling up in between my parents, I would always have the best sleep...*without* any nightmares or interruptions.

As the years passed, my parents tried to convince me that no monsters were living in my closet or under my bed. Even though I knew differently, soon I agreed and began to stay in my own bed. However, I always found myself sleeping with the bedcovers over my head and my eyes tightly shut. The nightmares never stopped and neither did the visits from the entity dwelling in my bedroom closet *(see Chapter Four)*. The themes of my nightmares were repetitive...sometimes even down to the smallest details. Flashes

The rock that was shown to me in my nightmares.

of skeletons were shown to me in some type of long wooden boxes and suddenly the skeletons would turn to ashes. There would also be dreams of dark figures fighting without ever making a sound and then I would see pieces of bones and skulls placed neatly on an odd shaped flat rock — a rock I would discover on our property in the woods later in my life.

These dreams tormented me. Sometimes, I would dream of more dark figures hiding in the corners of our upstairs hallway and two figures would always be on our staircase that led to the first floor of the house. Again, there was never any movement or sound. There were many more nightmares, but these were my recurring ones. This continued until the day I finally moved out of the house and on my own.

Experts say that one out of four kids suffers from nightmares. The phenomenon is believed to occur several times a week. Just like an adult's everyday life, a child's life can be very stressful — and that stress could cause some of the nightmares. If a family pet passes away, that is often a traumatic event or even the annual doctor's visit could be considered extremely taxing for a young child. Sometimes children worry about the smallest issues, but again that can cause nightmares for that child. What about the severe issues? An abusive home life or a parent's sudden passing could leave a child feeling unsafe or even abandoned. These are just a few examples of the causes that may be the reason for a child's nightmares.

What if there were no traumatizing incidents in the child's life? What would be the explanation if the child received a clean bill of health? Is the answer within the child's mind? Does the child just have an overactive imagination? Could the child be psychically gifted? Alternatively, should we perhaps ask the question, "What is truly lurking in my child's room?"

I suggest asking the child to talk about their nightmares; make sure the child knows that what he/she shares will not be shrugged off. Write down what the child is telling you and review the dreams each week to find a common trigger or issue. If the child feels the parent or parents are not listening, the child or children could withdraw and keep their experiences to themselves. This could cause medical issues down the road for the child, such as ulcers or something much worse. Thoughts of suicide could start to overwhelm the child's mind, thinking that suicide is the only way out or only solution to the problem. Understand that I am not saying he/she will indeed take such a dramatic route, but from time to time, this does happen.

The Adult's Experience

Night Terrors

Typically labeled a child's sleep disorder, night terrors in adults is not normal. However, some adults do experience them in the same fashion that kids do. The problem is that the older you get, the better the chance of injuring yourself or others around you. In the most severe form, the night terrors occur regularly and can result in an injury to the sufferer or the person's family.

In adults, the night terrors are not as much a matter of genetic predisposition, but most likely some form of psychological trauma. Adults suffering from night terrors commonly share characteristics with those who have been abused or are depressed, such as not showing their anger and taking it out on themselves, anxiety, the ability to ignore pain, and trouble retaining information or remembering specific events.

Although the symptoms are similar in both adult and children suffering night terrors, the treatment is very different. Due to the idea that most adult night terrors are caused by psychological damage done to the patient, they attend psychotherapy sessions and take anti-depression medication. This typically relieves the issue. Also a change in diet and behavioral modification when it comes to sleep times and regulating patterns often helps to bring the terrors under some control or at least diminish their frequency.

Nightmares

Adults experience nightmares too! If my body becomes too hot from a heavy blanket or the summer heat or if I try to take naps during the afternoon, this action will actually induce nightmares for me. I have had some of my most vivid and frightening dreams during these times as an adult. However, these dreams have a very different feel than those nightmares I experienced as a child. The nightmares I had as a child were my everyday reality...unless I was sleeping outside the home — that is the only time I would experience a restful night's sleep without any type of dream. The dreams I have today are just that...dreams of everyday stress or upsets that I encounter during that day.

Like children, adults suffer from extreme stress and trauma. With adulthood comes more responsibilities, such as family, bills, work, health, and everything else in-between. With all of these issues weighing on our minds, I am surprised that any of us get a good night's sleep at all!

Another well-known subject that causes nightmares in both children and adults is called Post-Traumatic Stress Disorder. This disorder is caused by a traumatic event such as a violent crime, a serious accident, being in the military/war, or experiencing a natural disaster. All these issues can trigger severe cases of nightmares and insomnia.

HYPNAGOGIC HALLUCINATIONS

Hypnagogia is a term that was first uttered by French psychologist Alfred Maury to give a name to that time between wakefulness and sleep. It is derived from the Greek húpnos, which means sleep, and agōg, which means to lead away or abduct. You can find many early references to hypnagogia, although it was not called that at the time. Maury simply put a name to what people had already known for centuries...that the time between waking and sleeping was powerful.

Aristotle looked for the truth in the hypnagogic state. He deemed that when in this grey area, you do not dream — *you cannot dream* — for you are not asleep and therefore not dreaming. He also asserted that because the body was there, so is the consciousness to some degree, and that even while we are asleep, our mind still is active and that is what may be part of the presentation during the hypnagogic state. Aristotle also speaks of the phantoms figures that often present themselves while someone is in this state and talks of the feeling of imminent fear surrounding the victim:

> "That what we here urge is true, i.e. that there are such presentative movements in the sensory organs, any one may convince himself, if he attends to and tries to remember the affections we experience when sinking into slumber or when being awakened. He will sometimes, in the moment of awakening, surprise the images which present themselves to him in sleep, and find that they are really but movements lurking in the organs of sense. And indeed some very young persons, if it is dark, though looking with wide open eyes, see multitudes of phantom figures moving before them, so that they often cover up their heads in terror. From all this, then, the conclusion to be drawn is, that the dream is a sort of presentation, and, more particularly, one which occurs in sleep; since the phantoms just mentioned are not dreams, nor is any other a dream which presents itself when the sense-perceptions are in a state of freedom."
>
> ~ On Dreams by Aristotle,
> Written 350 B.C.E

Edgar Allan Poe took a decidedly different direction with his hallucinations — he used them creatively, writing them into his stories and other works.

> "There is, however, a class of fancies, of exquisite delicacy, which are not thoughts, and to which, as yet, I have found it absolutely impossible to adapt language. I use the word fancies at random, and merely because I must use some word; but the idea commonly attached to the term is not even remotely applicable to the shadows of shadows in question. They seem to me rather psychal than intellectual. They arise in the soul (alas, how rarely!) only at its epochs of most intense tranquillity—when the bodily and mental health are in perfection–and at those mere points of time where the confines of the waking world blend with those of the world of dreams. I am aware of these "fancies" only when I am upon the very brink of sleep, with the consciousness that I am so. I have

satisfied myself that this condition exists but for an inappreciable point of time—yet it is crowded with these "shadows of shadows"; and for absolute thought there is demanded time's endurance.

These "fancies" have in them a pleasurable ecstasy, as far beyond the most pleasurable of the world of wakefulness, or of dreams, as the Heaven of the Northman theology is beyond its Hell. I regard the visions, even as they arise, with an awe which, in some measure moderates or tranquillises the ecstasy—I so regard them, through a conviction (which seems a portion of the ecstasy itself) that this ecstasy, in itself, is of a character supernal to the Human Nature—is a glimpse of the spirit's outer world; and I arrive at this conclusion—if this term is at all applicable to instantaneous intuition—by a perception that the delight experienced has, as its element, but the absoluteness of novelty. I say the absoluteness—for in the fancies—let me now term them psychal impressions—there is really nothing even approximate in character to impressions ordinarily received. It is as if the five senses were supplanted by five myriad others alien to mortality."

~ Edgar Allan Poe
Marginalia Graham's Magazine
March 1846

Now you see two completely different views; Aristotle claimed people were terrified of their hypnagogic hallucinations and Poe found them to be the height of spirituality and ecstasy. Here is the difference: when we are unconsciously going into a hypnagogic state, oftentimes a mild case of sleep paralysis may also be present; for others it can be more intense and the feelings of fear that are brought on by this other phenomena can turn this possibly positive event into a negative and frightful experience. You see that in essence the grey area is meant to put us into a state of deep relaxation that allows us to drift into slumber.

There is a way to get a handle on it though and use it to your benefit! With lucid dreaming, which is when *you are aware* that you are dreaming, it is possible to take control within the dream. Why would you want to lucid dream? Why not! When people first realize they are in a dream and that no matter what they do there will be no social, psychological, or physical consequences, it is a freedom that will soon become irreplaceable. It is also one of the best tools for dealing with nightmares; because you realize no physical harm can come to you, it allows you to face your fear within the nightmare. For example:

> "One young man dreamt of being pursued by a lion. When he had no place left to run, he realized he was dreaming and called to the lion to 'come and get him.' The challenge turned into a playful wrestling match, and the lion became a sexy woman."
>
> ~ Night Light (1.4, 1989)

So is hypnagogic hallucination a help or a threat? I believe it is a help; it is a tool that can be used to unlock creativity, learn about the self, and have a lot of fun in the dream state. Why be on the sidelines when you can play in the field? There are no specific signs for these hallucinations. Many modern scientists believe that they are nothing more than the mind trying to dump excess information. Although, if you look back and really study the many accounts of people and researchers who have reached the hypnagogic state, you will find that, much like dreams, these hallucinations may contain more wisdom than even our own conscious minds could dream of.

SLEEP PARALYSIS

This is a subject that even I come across from time to time while working on cases dealing with the paranormal. In fact, while writing this book, a woman contacted me scared out of her mind thinking she was being physically attacked by either an evil demonic force or a negative spirit when, in fact, she was dealing with a case of sleep paralysis. The client felt an unknown presence standing beside her bed while she slept and would suddenly wake up, feeling as if she was being attacked by this presence. She was convinced that a demonic force was in her bedroom, but would only attack her at night while she was sleeping. I explained that demonic entities do not just attack a person or home at night, but continue to do so even during the day. I found no evidence of a demonic haunting and nothing solid that could convince me her experiences were even from the spirit world.

The only experiences she could remember were feelings of being pressed down on her chest while she was sleeping and seeing a shadow of someone floating above her and quickly disappearing. When I discussed the possible cause of her issues, she felt a sigh of relief. The next day I emailed her the name of a few sleep centers in the area where she lived and she assured me that this was definitely the route she would take. Since then, the client has seen a specialist dealing with sleep paralysis disorder and now enjoys a safe, non-disturbing sleep.

Nightmares, night terrors, and sleep paralysis are such terrible issues to deal with, but these sleep disorders are not unusual, especially if one is under extreme stress or trauma. Sleep paralysis is actually one symptom of a much larger problem: narcolepsy. The two main indicators are excessive fatigue during the day and abnormal REM sleep. Sleep paralysis on its own has actually established itself in the paranormal community, as many paranormal investigators are now realizing that this disorder could be the cause of many of their clients' experiences.

Sleep paralysis has also been called the "Hag Syndrome" and perhaps could be where the original origins and legends of the evil entity known as Incubus/Succubus came from. People with this disorder will experience the feeling of being unable to move... being forced down in the bed and not allowed to move or get up because someone or something is pressing on their chest. Now these are just a few of the most common symptoms that someone might experience. Overcoming an episode is difficult, but not impossible to do. First, remain calm above all else. Second, this may be scary at first, but try to let the feelings flow. Third, try small movements with parts of your body such as toes and fingers. This will make it easier to come out of the sleep paralysis and eventually the body will be allowed to move freely and back to normal. If this happens several times a week, please call your local doctor. Sometimes medications will help or the doctor will refer a sleep center to monitor your sleeping patterns.

A woman falls prey to the incubus and succubus. The weight upon the chest is a common symptom of sleep paralysis.

Chapter Three:
VORTEXES, PORTALS, AND OTHER GATEWAYS

I love speaking at lectures, as it is an opportunity for me to share the knowledge I have gleaned over the years and sometimes even learn things myself. Once I was asked the question, "I heard that when you leave a door or window open it actually makes it easier for a spirit to enter the house. Is that true?" The answer is...*absolutely, positively no.* However, there are doorways that these entities can utilize to get between parallel universes. This includes the home. Think of it like "Alice in Wonderland": there you are making a daisy chain and the next thing you know you see a rabbit and decide to follow it down the little rabbit hole (a portal). As a result, you fall into a completely different world. I have personally never been in a portal, but I hope that it is as easy a ride as the one Alice went in.

Portals are something I have to keep in mind when conducting a paranormal investigation. There are some portals called "dynamic portals" that appear and disappear. They are not completely open, but can still allow energies to pass through. Animals, such as cats and dogs, are a great tool in locating portals and gateways; some paranormal groups, when they suspect a portal, will actually bring in a dog to "sniff" the portal out. From time to time, I find myself called into cases where portals are the main issues of the haunting... the spirits are coming and going just like a revolving door. Beckah, a psychic medium I have worked with, is a pro at finding these types of doorways; she uses her abilities to see the energy of the portals. Once the location has been established, Beckah closes the portals and clears the home of any other spirits. To see a portal in person is amazing. The only way I can best describe it is like seeing heat rays wafting off a newly tarred road under the hot summer sun.

Good vs. Bad Portals

The other most commonly asked question I get is: "What makes a portal a good portal and a bad portal, bad?" This is a great question; many people will tell you that there are positive and negative forces and that the world is based on polarities. According to Einstein, these individuals would be right. Unfortunately, I have not seen any "Negative Entities Only" signs hanging on any portals lately. Talking about portals, vortexes, and gateways opens up a whole assortment of problems. There may be no "Negative Entities Only" sign hanging, but if these portals do lead to a parallel universe, then who is to say that some of these beings are not just downright evil.

For a long time portals have been considered "fixed" doorways — the doorway does not move around; it stays where it has been since the earth was made. If one looks at cases like the Bridgewater Triangle in Bridgewater, Massachusetts, there have been rumors of portals and boogeyman like activity. Kids have been claiming for years that they see people in their rooms; parents talk about hearing footsteps in the hall or passing by the spirits of Native Americans dressed in full regalia on the hiking trails; there have been UFO sightings, and mysterious creatures are prevalent in the area. Now you may ask what makes me think it might be a portal? Good question. There has been a heck of a lot of bloodshed across the globe, yet this one place does not consist of one or two isolated hauntings. No, it is the *entire* area and it has been happening for centuries. Even the Native Americans held a passionate respect for this area. They knew that here was a place they could get in touch with their loved ones and where their ancestors spoke to them. Therefore, the Natives regarded it as sacred. This information is one of many final nails in the coffin of my theory. No, the

Bridgewater Triangle is not a mass of individual hauntings, but a *mass haunting* caused by an individual portal. It is a matter of time, how many cases, and the frequency and consistency of the reports... *Bridgewater meets all of those criteria.*

Science is always making great strides. No longer is it a question of if there are parallel universes to our own, but more a matter of what or where are they? Unfortunately, it seems that the portals that we generally come across are not one hundred percent active yet. Yes, they can let energies pass through, but not solid objects. Maybe we just have not figured out how to harness the ability to do it yet or to activate the portals completely.

As I had said earlier, this chapter opens up a whole assortment of problems for me. I love to theorize and think of the infinite possibilities....

VORTEXES

The Good, the Bad, & the Boogeyman

Vortexes are very different from portals, but again, people feel there are bad vortexes and good vortexes. Honestly, I do not know, although through research and my own experiences I have a theory. I believe that they are neither good nor bad; they are simply pure energy. No spirits or any other entity will pass through a vortex because the energies are not on the same level. I do think that there is a positive and negative force though. Think of it like being on a rollercoaster: when you go up fast, it is fun and exhilarating; when you go down fast, your stomach is in your chest. One is fun; the other can be quite frightening.

If you ever go to Sedona, Arizona, locals believe the area has several vortexes. Peter A. Sanders, Jr., a vortex expert in the Sedona area, honors graduate of Massachusetts' MIT, and author of *Scientific Vortex Information* and *You Are Psychic!*, classifies vortexes this way:

"Vortex sites are enhanced energy locations that facilitate prayer, meditation, mind/body healing, and exploring your relationship with your Soul and the divine. They are neither electric nor magnetic (although these words are often used to describe the vortexes, along with the other nomenclature such as masculine or feminine sites). The explanation for vortexes lies more at the boundaries of known science, rather than in electromagnetic descriptions or gender related labels. Recently the PBS program Nova featured a breakthrough in physics called "String Theory" (also known as super-strings) that is revolutionizing all of science on the same order of magnitude that Einstein's discoveries did in the early 1900s. The key spiritual implications of super-strings is that the world's top scientists agree that all things exist in a minimum of 10 or more dimensions. Simply stated Vortex sites are locations having energy flows in those deeper dimensions that the Soul can soar on. Upflow Vortexes (also called electric or masculine sites) have energy flows that help you soar to higher spiritual perspectives. They enhance prayers or meditations for blending with the Universe, feeling one with the divine, or facing a problem from a Soul level. Inflow Vortexes (also called magnetic or feminine) have energy flows that help you go inward. In them you will be more successful with meditations or prayers about your life purpose or how to heal hurts in your past. There are also Combination Vortexes that have aspects of both energies. These allow the seeker to experience more advanced or in depth spiritual skills and meditations."

According to Peter's theory and that of others like him, they see there being a spiritual proponent that can be gained through the vortex — that it can actually help you attain enlightenment and increased psychic ability. How does this work? Well, there is what we call vibrational levels. Think of it like a tuning fork; they each come in different notes and produce a different energy. When you hit a tuning fork, it vibrates. This shows that aside from just the sound it makes it is producing the energy needed. Our energy vibrations are low on the spectrum. Vortexes, however, go through the spectrum of energy vibrations, from super high to super low. In Sedona, there are believed to be four main vortexes (although some residents will tell you the whole place is a giant vortex) operating at high energy levels. Because it is vibrating at this high energy level, when you are meditating with it, on it, or near it, you are tapping into that energy causing your own energy to reach the same level as the vortex for a short space of time.

It is believed that there are actually twelve major vortexes evenly distributed across the planet. These were first described, mapped, and dubbed Vile Vortices by Ivan T. Sanderson, a naturalist and paranormal investigator. His first use of the now iconic term was in his article "The Twelve Devil's Graveyards Around the World" (*Saga Magazine*, 1972). One of them is the now the infamous Bermuda Triangle. There is also the Devil's Sea Triangle, which is off the coast of Japan between Iwo Jima and Marcus Island — many ships and planes have been lost there for unknown reasons. It has gotten so bad that Japanese officials have designated this as a danger zone. I read about it originally in *Anti-Gravity and the World Grid* by David Hatcher Childress, in which he says:

> "Another area of continuing disappearances and mysterious time-warps is the Devil's Sea located east of Japan between Iwo Jima and Marcus Island. Here events have become so sinister that the Japanese government has officially designated the area a danger zone. Sanderson theorized that the tremendous hot and cold currents crossing his most active zones might create the electromagnetic gymnastics affecting instruments and vehicles. His theory is now being balanced against several."

The mapping done by Sanderson really blew things out of the water; it was talked about in the paranormal community for quite some time and is still a hot topic to this day. However, he was not the only one to devise this system of mapping:

> "The ten regions, says Sanderson, are symmetrically situated around the globe; five above and five below at equal distances from the equator. Had the American investigator thought to add two more points, at the North and South poles, say the Russians, his scheme would have precisely coincided with the model which they have adopted."
>
> ~ "Planetary Grid," *New Age Journal*, 1975

So, vortexes are very different from portals, although I do believe the word *vile* may be a little too strong. However, these anomalies certainly can throw things out of whack. At the same time you have other vortexes, perhaps of a weaker energy, that can help to heal and bring fulfillment and peace back into our lives. The Bermuda Triangle and Devil's Sea Triangle still give no firm answers as to what is causing the disappearances, where these ships and planes are going, or if they will ever appear in another place or even another time.

MiRROR, MiRROR...

Ever since I can remember, I have always had an issue with mirrors. I have never liked having them in my bedroom and do not have one even today in the room, but growing up my bureau — the one that came out of my parents' storage above the garage for my new bedroom...the bedroom that had Fire Face living in my closet — had a large mirror attached to it. Shadows and apparitions seemed to come and go through this mirror, but not all the time.

My fear of mirrors became almost like a phobia... I remember sleeping over a friend's and being so terrified because of the mirror that it took me almost three hours to fall asleep. She had a full-length mirror that took up the front of their closet door, which I just happened to be sleeping in front of. There was nothing paranormal about her mirror, but it did make my mind wonder and think about the possibilities. Mirrors, like water, are reflective and these reflective surfaces have been credited for hundreds, even thousands of years for showing people the future and connecting with spirits. Scrying in reflective surfaces is an age-old practice that dates back to the times when they made mirrors of carved obsidian in 6500 BCE. John Dee, Queen Elizabeth's famous astrologer and alchemist, had an obsidian scrying mirror; he was then later given credit for predicting an assassination attempt on King James in 1605 after a scrying session. One of these obsidian mirrors now resides in the British Museum. When they opened the bag holding the mirror, they were pleased to find a piece of parchment inside of it, written by Sir Horace Walpole, a famous English antiquarian who acquired the mirror in 1771. The note began with:

> "The Black Stone into which Dr. Dee used to call his spirits. Kelly was Dr. Dee's Associate and is mentioned with this very stone in "Hudibras," a satirical poem written by Samuel Butler and first published in 1664. Kelly did all his feats upon The Devil's Looking-glass, a Stone."

Dee and Kelley went on to conduct even more experiments in occult research. Unfortunately, even with the impact they made on modern occultists, Dee died penniless, forced to sell most of his prized occult possessions (if I only had a time machine!) in order to support himself and his daughter who stayed with him till he died.

John Dee's mirror may not scare you, but some of the superstitions surround these reflective objects might. There, of course, are many superstitions that can be found throughout history applying to the boogeyman and the mirror. One in particular caught my interest. It hearkens back to the Victorian era when spirituality was at its height and honoring the dead was at its most dramatic. Superstition of the time stated that if someone died in a particular room and there were mirrors in it...the mirrors MUST be covered. Otherwise, the deceased person's soul might have become trapped in the mirror and not be able to cross over to the other side.

I have always been a supporter of occultism; we are like the scientists of spirituality and much like any other science you need to get an education before you go in the lab and experiment. In the past, I have been called into cases where someone who is just starting out in the occult field decided to "try something wicked cool" and create a portal in their mirror. These mirrors are made for the sole purpose of contacting spirits from the other realms (these magical mirrors must have the proper symbols and text on certain areas of the mirror). There is a fine line between controlling and being controlled when you work in the occult. When you open a portal even with the best of intentions, you really do not know where the portal leads or who is going to come out. Subversive spirits are known for being sly and taking control of the occultist when they let their guard down. Many times, I have seen this happen and soon an occult expert must be called in to "close" the mirror and any portals that may have been made around the area where the mirror was used. This can become a dangerous situation for the occult expert because there are those times when more than just spirits come though those portals; sometimes demonic entities will take this as an invitation to come through into our realm.

Buying antiques is a huge passion of mine; I love to find those old and rare occult items. However, these antiques could have spirits or other types of entities attached to them, especially mirrors. I never allow an antique into my home unless it is "cleansed" first. One way to cleanse an item is to burn white sage and allow the smoke to smother the item from top to bottom, inside and out. This action will detach the spirit or entity and force them away from the home or area you are saging. It is important to remember when you are bringing used and antique items into your home that they at one time or another belonged to someone else and that someone may still want them.

Section Two:

PERSONAL EXPERIENCES... OF A STRANGE KIND

Chapter Four:
TALES OF TERROR

In our everyday life, we go to work and we hang out with friends and loved ones. Nevertheless, sometimes when each of us returns to our homes at night, something unseen to others is lurking in our home or bedroom. Feelings of fear overcome our bodies... Feelings of being watched when no one is there fills our senses...

The doors are locked, the blinds are down, and the home alarm is on...*yet there is something wrong*. Who is there? Why is my child scared to sleep in their bedroom at night? Is it our own imaginations running wild? At first, that just might be the case, but as the night goes on, our minds are changed and the terror begins. I have dealt with many paranormal cases in which the client swears that the "Boogeyman" is haunting them or terrorizing their children at night. Any case that involves children is a top priority for me; most children are psychically open and can be very susceptible to some form of spirit attack.

Our society labels "Spirits" or "Demonic Entities" as the Boogeyman and, for some reason, this might be more believable to the everyday person. Spirits are everywhere and always around each of us; some are loved ones that have crossed over and stop in to visit with our children or to make sure a sick family member is recuperating properly after an illness or a surgery. There are those cases where a spirit is "stuck" or "grounded" and just needs help in crossing over or even just to share their tragic story with us; the latter is a kind of healing for some spirits and makes it easier to see the "light" when crossing over. Sometimes we may encounter more than just a past family member; sometimes we may cross paths with something more dangerous with an evil intent behind the haunting.

TYPES OF SPIRITS

Here is a list of the most common types of spirits and entities that a person could at some point in their life encounter.

Spirit Guides

These are spirits that can help with direction in a person's life. In some cases the spirit guide can be a past loved one or a friend who has crossed over, or even a higher being of light, such as Angels or positive beings of light.

Visiting

These spirits all have been to the other side and is typically family or a spirit that is attached to the land or building for a specific reason (such as loved the home or had fond memories of the area). Some spirits are just checking in on a sick relative or giving comfort to a troubled family member. These spirits are not harmful, but on occasion, the spirit might try to make contact by appearing in dreams or even dispersing a certain fragrance into the air that reminds a person of that passed relative or friend.

It is not uncommon for me to get called into a spirit haunting case and for it to be a spirit in visitation that the client has confused with a grounded or negative spirit. Spirits in visitation may try to get attention. Oftentimes it is because they want to warn you of danger or something coming up that could impact your life. Let them know that you know they are around to help or because they are just playful.

Grounded

Unlike those spirits that are just in visitation, these spirits have not been to the other side yet, typically for reasons of fear, guilt, anger, unresolved issues, or because a quick death occurred (such as suicide, murder, or an accidental death). In some cases, the spirits may become possessive of a certain place or object and will not cross over willingly. If this happens, then I suggest calling in a professional psychic medium to help the spirit cross over.

Attached

This can either be a spirit in visitation or is grounded that has become attached to a person, place, or even an object. In some cases, these spirits just need to share their story with a living person to move on.

Once, while I was still a Corrections Officer, I experienced a spirit that attached to me. I had been posted that day at the hospital to watch a sick inmate. The day went smoothly and I headed home, which was just down the road from the hospital. The spirit of a person who had passed away during an operation attached itself to me and followed me home.

Beckah, who is a wonderful and gifted psychic medium, was waiting for me to come home because we had an investigation that night. We had been talking and did not notice this spirit at first. Suddenly, the back door opened and slammed hard. The spirit felt it was not being heard or noticed, so it needed to find another way to get our attention. Beckah realized it was an attachment and helped the male spirit cross over. Beckah told me after the spirit had crossed that he wanted me to know that his mother always said, "If you ever get lost, find an officer and they will help you find your way back home." The spirit did just that.

Negative Spirits

It is difficult at first glance to determine what type of spirit may be occupying your home. However, when it comes to negative spirits, these types are not usually timid in the least and want you to know they are there. Typically they like to use intimidation tactics that worked during their lifetime: forcing negative feelings on you, locking you in rooms, poltergeist activity...sometimes even to the point of physical harm. These people were mean in life and continue the abusive behavior even after death.

With a negative spirit, unlike with the others, if you tell them to quit bothering you, instead of decreasing the activity it will increase threefold. They do not like to be told what to do and you could end up in a hostile situation. Your best bet would be to get a professional team or medium in to deal with the negative spirit. Usually it ends with the psychic or cleric having to give the entity their eviction notice.

Angelic Spirits

These are spirits of pure light and are here to help guide and protect humans. St. Augustine explained angels the best:

> "The name Angel refers to their office, not their nature. You ask the name of this nature, it is spirit; you ask its office, it is that of an Angel, which is a messenger."

These, along with Elemental and Demonic entities, make up the class of inhuman spirits that have never touched the Earth as a living organism, whether it is human, animal, or plant. Angelic spirits can actually be very useful. As I said, they are here to guide us, but at the same time each Angel has a specialty. For example, Archangel Raphael can be used to help with success in business and all matters of the spoken word and Archangel Michael can help with protection (both during travel and at any time when feeling threatened) and you can also pray to him to help find lost or stolen property. I feel that even though you may never see an angel with your own two eyes, every time you pray to one you share an encounter with its energy, if not his or her physical form.

Elemental Spirits

These are spirits of the elements, such as earth, fire, air, and water. These are very powerful entities, although they would be considered under the listing of inhuman spirits because they have never been a living, breathing organism. They are not the demonic entities that many people confuse them for. Elementals feed on energy and wreak havoc within the scope of that element. For example, a spirit of the element water could turn on faucets, blow up pipes, and cause flooding. How does one come across such a spirit? By disturbing or destroying forests, throwing toxins or waste products into bodies of water, or landscaping an area that is a dwelling place or home of an Elemental spirit. It is rare to stumble across Elemental spirits, but it can certainly happen.

Demonic Entities

These are the worst of the worst; these entities are made from pure negative energy and are most commonly called demons or diabolical spirits. These are entities that have never "touched" the earth as a human. They have eons of knowledge on us and often use underhanded tactics to gain an invitation (such as playing with a spirit board unprotected or using a form of summoning a demon for personal gain) to mess with and destroy the human race. Demonic entities are looking to cause chaos wherever possible and to break down the "will" of the person who gave permission or, unknowingly, an invitation.

Homes can also be considered possessed by demonic entities; objects and, far worse, humans can also become possessed. This stage of an attack might or does call for an exorcism to be performed. Demonic attacks are rare to experience, but they can happen. Do NOT try to remove this type of entity on your own — call in a professional demonologist or local priest to deal with the dangerous issue.

FiRE FACE

This story is one that haunts my memories even to this day — this is my own story of the terror I experienced as a child. This is the story of my "Boogeyman," which I named Fire Face when I was young.

Let us travel back in time when I was very little, around five or six years old. My original bedroom was rather small with a single bed next to one wall and a dresser with a large mirror attached pushed up against another wall. A small closet held my good clothes built into the corner of the room. My mother felt that when I got a little older I would move into my brother's bedroom and he would move into my old room. She always believed girls needed more space than boys. I think she felt that way because she grew up with three brothers and didn't have that privacy as a young girl herself. My brother was about three years older than I was and was rarely home due to being in Little League during the summer and on the Ski Racing team during the winter.

In my book *Devils and Demonology in the 21st Century*, I shared for the first time my experience seeing the entity that later I would call "Fire Face" in my brother's bedroom while playing one early morning with him. Now I will share even more details about living in an extremely haunted house.

The entity was large in build with broad shoulders. No facial appearances could be seen; *no* eyes, eyelids, nose, ears, hair, or mouth...nothing. All that could be seen was an ash type texture that covered the entity's whole body. The entity just stood there in my brother's bedroom doorway as my brother and I played with his Hot Wheels cars on the floor behind one of the single beds that were in the bedroom. (There were two single beds; one my brother slept in and the other for company). For some odd reason, I turned and looked directly at the entity standing in the doorway. Of course, as any child would have done at that moment, I ran screaming at the top of my lungs. (My brother, who at the time had been facing a different direction, never spoke of the incident.)

This is my brother and I around the age when I started having interactions with the entity "Fire Face."

I must have been so scared with fright that I ran right *through* the entity and down the hall where my mother had come running, meeting me half way. I remember she was still in her red zipped up night robe wondering what was going on or what my brother had done to me this time.

The Dreaded Bedroom…

A few years later, my mother moved me into that bedroom, even though I had barely been in it since the incident happened with Fire Face, and my brother got my old room. He was not pleased at all by this. My brother knew how scared I was by "Fire Face" and the bedroom closet. However, being an older brother, he loved to tease and harass me. He would throw my favorite toys on the top shelf of the closet and, if I wanted to get the toys, I had to go all the way back in the corner of the closet to retrieve them. My father had built a shelf that started half way in the closet and ended in the dark corner inside.

However, "Fire Face" not only terrorized me during the day, but also at night when I tried to fall asleep. The deep breathing at night bothered me the most, for that meant "Fire Face" was approaching my bed. Closer, closer, and my eyes would close shut, tighter and tighter. I remember feeling my blanket and sheet being pushed closer to my body and face. Sometimes, when I felt very brave, which was not very often, I quickly threw the bedcovers off me and saw just darkness standing before me. I turned my bedside light on and saw the closet door now closed. Nevertheless, just earlier that night, the sound of someone or something had in fact opened the closet door. Slowly the sound of the closet door handle would move and a sound of the door opening was heard. My bedroom door was always open, and sometimes during those brave moments at night, I could see the dark figures heading down the hall and straight to my room. The brave moment over, back under the bedcovers I would hide.

Our cat, Buttons, would never enter my bedroom, even when she was a kitten. She would hiss and scratch at me wildly if I even dared to try to carry her to my bedroom. Strangely, though, we could carry her all through the other bedrooms and never have an issue. This bedroom started to strangely affect my whole family. My father, who always said goodnight to me in person while I was sleeping in the smaller room, would never come near my new bedroom. My brother became obsessed with breaking my toys and throwing them into the haunted closet. My mother became obsessed with ripping my posters off my walls — never mind that these are the same posters that she bought for me and helped me hang on my wall. Then, when my mother stepped out into the hallway, she seemed a bit confused and then was back to her happy self.

The air in the bedroom was always thick; it was like hitting a brick wall everytime I entered the bedroom. I had three normal sized windows and one small window, so the outside air was circulating in the room. Even when my friends would come over and hang out in my bedroom sudden verbal fights would happen without any real reason as to why the fight started in the first place. It was as if the "room" or entity only wanted me there. Soon I became more withdrawn from my family and friends, and my room became the center of my world when I was home.

Today, I understand from working in the paranormal field that I was being "attacked" by the entity, but being young, I knew nothing about the paranormal or just what exactly was going on in my bedroom.

The Whole Property is Haunted...

There were so many occurrences that I would love to share about growing up in this haunted home, but I will cover the most intense experiences I went through. The most intense situations occurred within the shell of the house, my bedroom in particular; however, there was also activity outside the home. I do not believe that a spirit followed me or that there was an attachment of that sort, I think that there was a connection to the land. This included inside both the house and the rest of our property, as well as some of the neighbors' houses.

When playing outside in our large yard, which was bordered by some small woods in the back of our home, I always had the strong urge to play the game "war" and run around pretending I was getting shot at by the enemies that were hiding in the woods and behind the large rocks on the edge of our property. One time my mother had bought my brother and I some fake Indian tomahawks to play with. I was outside in our yard alone and placed the tomahawk down on the ground next to me while I tied my shoelace. I never saw my toy tomahawk again. Being a child, I just did not think twice about the missing item and continued playing outside, thinking maybe I would come across it later that day. My tomahawk never resurfaced. Sure, some individuals would just chalk this experience up to a child losing a toy outside while playing. I would normally have to agree, but other strange occurrences began to happen as well....

Attached to our home in the back was a slate patio with stairs that led down the lawn to another driveway. Sometimes the patio would become covered with toads and other times — and these instances were not related because they happened months apart — there would be large amounts of gardener snakes. After that, my mother called her dear friend, Father B, in to bless our home. This would not be the first or last time Father B would come and bless our home, and our home — inside and outside — would become peaceful for a short time.

After a while, more activity came in the house at full force, including my name being called in my father's voice when no one other than I was home. I would come running downstairs to greet my father, only to find no one there. The voices were always male and always in my father's voice — the voice would call me by the name Katie Ann and my father was the only one who ever called me by my first and middle name — never female and never in my mother's or brother's voice. Missing or broken objects (candleholders and my mother's rosary beads went missing and were never found again) became a regular occurrence in the house and lights would suddenly turn on and off downstairs when no one was in the room. Sounds of muffled talking and loud bangs were also common.

Once in the early morning hours, a burglar had made his way onto our patio. We had no alarm systems in our homes back then, as most families living in the neighborhood never locked their doors at night. My whole family was woken up to the sounds of a man screaming out loud in fear and the sounds of someone running into the two patio chairs that were set up outside. The next morning my father checked the whole property of our house and found nothing wrong or anything that would have scared off the burglar. We never had a burglary issue before and never did after that.

The Breakdown of the Family....

Then my father's strange behavior began....

My father loved to hunt and could often be found hunting deer during the season. He was not a history buff by any means, but a couple of years after we moved into our house, he became obsessed with buying antique muskets and making lead pellets for them. This was something out of the norm for him to do.

He would spend hours down in the basement, just sitting there, making lead round pellets for his musket, which he never even used. Although, when it came time for the town's Bicentennial parade, my mother was very happy about my father's sudden pre-occupation with antique guns and weaponry, e only family that carried a real period musket in remember my father being very displeased about sket, but my mother eventually wore him down he finally said yes. My brother was excited about carry a "real gun" in the parade. I think it made up outfit he had to wear in front of his friends. The of this was that my father did not even participate in the parade or even dress up. This is a common event when spirits start attacking each person in the home or even tries to influence the individual through certain actions...like the actions of my father.

My home had become turned upside down by these entities, as sudden arguments between all of us started to be an everyday

My mother, brother (with one of my father's antique muskets), and I dressed up for the Bicentennial Parade.

occurrence. Fire Face became more active in my bedroom, slamming my bedroom door closed and then opening it so fast the door handle went into the wall and remained stuck. Dark figures seemed to dash around my room and into the hallway upstairs, being pushed while standing in my room started to happen more, sometimes even my hair would be pulled hard, and I would scream out. The nightmares became more intense and I soon started to only get a few hours sleep a night.

Father B. visited more often to bless our home, but even he became sick with a sudden illness (might not be related to my home, but seemed rather odd at the time) and stopped with the visits altogether to our home. My mother did continue her visits with Father B., but the visits were now at his church's office until the day he passed away after a long battle with stomach cancer. The stress of the situation took a hard toll on my family. My brother got older and moved out, my parents divorced, and I moved out at the age of eighteen. My mother began to lose her mind while remaining in the house alone. Five years passed and my mother sold the house due to the divorce agreement between her and my father, and soon after, she passed away.

The Tragic History....

While writing *Devils and Demonology in the 21st Century*, my research came up with some very interesting history facts of Natives being slaughtered by colonists and fighting on and around the property my family's house was built on. I uncovered a ton of history on the town of Goffstown, including the fact that parts of the town were built over unmarked graves of natives and other settlers; murders and suicides happening once the town was built; and sudden outbursts of fires in the homes, which killed several of the settlers. This is just a few of the historical facts of the small town where I grew up.

Today it is not surprising for me to get phone calls from somebody scared out of their wits. "Please help me...I think my house is haunted!" the voice would say. Where does the client live? You guessed it: Goffstown, New Hampshire. Is Fire Face still dwelling inside my old home? Yes, I have driven by the house several times later in my life and the feelings can still be felt seeping from the house. I did notice that the owners who bought my childhood home from my parents many years ago have become obsessed with renovating the property and are constantly adding more soil to the yard (a rather odd amount of soil to cover up the whole backyard and the second driveway). They have also added more bushes around the property of the house.

THE BABY MONITOR

When working in the paranormal, you always need to be ready for the unexpected, but there will be those cases that will take you by surprise. This was one of those cases. I was called to a townhouse where a family lived in fear of an entity that was tormenting their young daughter. Elizabeth was eleven years old; she was a very typical girl for her age. Being into the latest pop stars and caught between young adult and child, these childhood fears were what worried the parents. Elizabeth suddenly became fearful of her room and refused to sleep in it; it was all the way on the top floor with beautiful skylights and the ultimate teen desire…privacy. Nevertheless, Elizabeth was not making full use of it. Everyday she would hang out in her room talking with an unseen presence that seemed to hang out in the corner of her room, but then every night, she would run downstairs to her parents' room.

Elizabeth also had a baby sister who was four months old. She became very dedicated to her younger sibling, who also seemed to have issues, and could not fall asleep at night. The baby would wake up out of a sudden sleep and cry at all hours of the night, as though it were having nightmares or seeing something that scared her awake. It was never an issue when the children were outside the house: both the baby and Elizabeth slept peacefully at the grandmother's house. Mom and dad still had the baby monitor set up in the baby's room — the receiver was in the kitchen — when I got there for the investigation.

Beckah, who is a wonderful and gifted psychic medium, was also there with me during the investigation and did a walk-through of the home before the investigation started. Beckah headed right upstairs to the baby's room and then to Elizabeth's room. She commented right away on the heaviness of the air in both rooms. Beckah also noticed a male spirit in both of the children's bedrooms, and stated that this male spirit belonged to the original property and used to work there.

I always trust my psychic, but these homes were brand new and, while there may have been farmland in the past, I was not one hundred percent sure. I had not done much of anything for background at this point, as typically I will wait until after the investigation is completed and then go back to verify and delve deeper into the past of the property. Luckily, the couple knew the history of the property and were eager to share it. Prior to the townhouse being built, there were actually mills and one in particular had burned down. Three children, five men, and one woman died in the fire. The parents believed that this spirit was one of these men that Beckah was speaking about during her walk-through of the home.

I Can See You! I Can Hear You!

During the process of the investigation, I did spend a fair amount of time in Elizabeth's room, but little did I know that the focus would soon shift to the baby monitor. Beckah and a few other paranormal investigators were in the kitchen downstairs

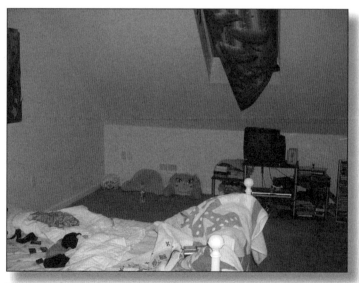

This was where we at first thought the activity emanated from. However, this room is directly above the baby's room — and that was where the activity was really taking place!

talking with the client when they began to hear noises and voices...
coming from the baby monitor.

Beckah ran upstairs and into the baby's room to determine
the source of the noises, as both children were not present during
the investigation. All of a sudden out of the baby monitor — and
keep in mind this is the one that transmits the noises and does
not receive them — a little girl giggled. Beckah called me on the
walkie-talkie and asked that I come downstairs right away.

Beckah asked me if anything occurred while I was upstairs
in the little girl's bedroom. Unfortunately, I could find nothing
to substantiate the little girl's claims at this point. I had not
experienced anything in the room except for some minor
temperature fluctuations, but that was not enough evidence to
convince me, just yet, of spiritual activity.

Baby monitors are very similar to walkie-talkies in that they
use radio waves to transmit signals from the transmitter to the
receiver; the only difference is with a baby monitor it works on
only one channel. Baby monitors can still be prone to interference
though; on more than one occasion I had been at a client's house
that had a baby monitor and heard another baby or a female
voice coming though. Sometimes interruptions come from a
CB radio or another monitor close by the home or area. The
only problem was that in this case there were no other monitors
close enough for the signals to cross. What also bothered me was
that the parents had never experienced any interference before
with the baby monitor, so my mind still was not sure that this
unexplained voice was in fact a spirit.

Beckah told me just what she had heard — a little girl giggling.
As we stood by the monitor in the bedroom, Beckah asked aloud,
"Little girl, if that was you, can you laugh again for me?" The
child's voice again came through clearly laughing and giggling
and then, right after the girl's voice, came a man's grunt.

Beckah and I looked at each other a little stunned. We expected
to hear the little girl. However, hearing the man's voice confirmed
the male spirit Beckah had felt so strongly earlier, but was this
male spirit intent on protecting or harming Elizabeth? Beckah

believed from what she felt that the man was a nuisance, very in and out in respect to his awareness of the family. "Sometimes he saw the family and other times he did not, but he always saw things as it used to be and not as they are," Beckah stated.

Beckah also believed that Elizabeth was sensitive to spirits because she acted like a "foghorn" to this particular spirit — her energy was giving off a feel of "I can see you! I can hear you!"

Elizabeth's mother also had run-ins with this male spirit, but she generally ignored his presence. This made him more frustrated than ever and at one point the mother said she had told him to cut it out and leave Elizabeth and the rest of the family alone. The spirit became frustrated and flung her purse — from the top of the refrigerator in the kitchen against the front door in the living room. This was the final straw for her and she finally told her husband they needed to get some outside help. He agreed, but when I walked out of the bedroom and went to the kitchen to talk with the family and they heard what I had to say about the investigation and evidence we had earlier experienced, it made their haunting very real. It was confirmed: it was not in their heads and their daughter was not simply acting out when she said she saw a man in her room... *Something really was there.*

The Conclusion....

I went back into the baby's room with the mother and father while Beckah and a couple of the other paranormal investigators went to Elizabeth's room with some dowsing wands and the K-II meter to see if they could get responses. In the baby's room, the little girl seemed to be the most prominent spirit. Speaking through the transmitter, which had four lights on it, as the volume of the noise coming through the transmitter got louder a light almost like those on an equalizer would register the level of noise. We asked the little girl to manipulate it for us, kind of like how we would with a K-II meter. At first there was absolute silence, but then the lights began to flicker back and forth.

You could only get up to Elizabeth's room through the baby's room; it was something like a finished attic space. The door to the stairs leading up to Elizabeth's room matched the closet doors exactly and easily could have been mistaken for one if you did not know it. I contacted Beckah on the walkie-talkie to let her know that I was getting responses.

"So are we," she stated. "The dowsing rods upstairs are going berserk, left right, spinning around, in response to questions."

I was extremely excited about this. Beckah had even taken a moment to ask the male spirit if he wanted help crossing over. The spirit gave an unequivocal yes answer through the dowsing wands. We all joined together in the baby's room and decided to ask for some knocks and bangs. We got some responses, particularly from the little girl, and once or twice from the man. Beckah decided that it might be beneficial to help both spirits cross over instead of just focusing on the male, even though he seemed to be causing most of the issues.

Since Beckah had cleared (helping spirits cross over) the home, Elizabeth and her little sister both sleep in their own bedroom comfortably every night. Peace has found its way back into the house again, and there have been no reports of any paranormal activity since the investigation.

The baby's room... The entrance to the stairway that led to her older sister Elizabeth's room can be seen.

IN PIECES

One day while I was in my office working on another paranormal case, the phone rang and on the other end was a woman, who, in a frantic voice, asked if I do exorcisms. My eyebrows lifted with interest. "Yes," I replied.

"I think my daughter might need one," the woman said back in a worried voice.

I asked for the full details as to just what exactly her daughter was experiencing. The mother knew most of the details, but did not live with her daughter and son-in-law. Her daughter was having terrible nightmares and having sudden visions of a fire burning in her apartment; it seemed so real to the daughter that in the middle of the night she even tried to put the fire out until her husband told her there was no fire. The kitchen cabinets began to open and suddenly slam shut, a shadow of a woman was seen near a corner of the bedroom, and they were experiencing extreme cold spots especially near one area of the floor in the bedroom. The daughter would feel very anxious everytime she entered the kitchen area and sudden screams in a woman's voice could be heard in the couple's bedroom. The daughter's mother did not want to waste any time and asked how soon I could meet with her and the daughter. Turns out the daughter just lived across the river from my house and, since I wasn't available the next day, we agreed on a time for the day after.

Beckah, a psychic medium who I work closely with on most of my paranormal cases, needed to be there for the meeting and the investigation. The information, which was given to me, seemed to lean more towards spirits than any type of demonic influence. Beckah and I are very skeptical about a case until we can gather all the facts and evidence before making any type of conclusion. In addition, I could not wait to see just what Beckah could discover during her walk-through of the apartment. Psychics often walk around the area, gathering information using impressions from the energy of a home, and communicating with entities that may reside there. To date, this is one of the most traumatic spirit cases I have ever worked on and you will soon find out why.

A Bad Feeling....

When Beckah and I arrived at the client's apartment, Beckah right away commented on how she DID NOT want to go inside the large white building that stood before us. "The feelings here make my stomach hurt," she said.

Yet, inside we went. The door to the client's apartment was already open and standing in the doorway was a scared looking young couple.

While I was getting the paranormal equipment and video camcorder out of the case, Beckah was already heading straight for the couple's bedroom. I quickly followed and began recording Beckah's walk-through. Right away, she noticed a strong spirit of a woman that was "grounded" and needed help crossing over to the other side.

A view from the living room into the client's bedroom... Beckah was drawn here as soon as we entered the apartment.

"No one is listening," Beckah stated, adding in a very low voice, "A woman was brutally tortured and murdered in this room. She was kept in this room for several days before this man stabbed her to death over and over and then raped her."

My own stomach at this point started to turn. Beckah also talked about how the spirit of the murdered victim felt abandoned and dirty; the spirit felt that the killer did not get what he deserved. I asked Beckah what the spirit meant by that comment. "I feel like the killer is locked up somewhere and will be locked up for a long time, but he feels no remorse or guilt for the murder," she said.

Before we moved on to the living room, Beckah also picked up on another female spirit. This woman died by smoke inhalation during the early 1900s and had crossed over, but used to live in the apartment and liked to visit on occasion. Each spirit did not see each other, for the time periods were much different; the murdered victim died in the late 1990s.

A Tragic End....

Now in the living room, we all stood, waiting to hear more from the murdered victim.

Beckah stated how the woman's body was dragged from the bedroom, across the living room, and into the kitchen. Suddenly the temperature felt rather warm and the air became thick and heavy to breathe. Beckah also mentioned people living in this apartment would suffer from terrible nightmares, but added how the murdered victim just needed her story to be heard. Then something I just did not expect came from Beckah's lips. "She was ripped apart...she keeps saying that she was ripped apart," Beckah said in a loud voice. I do not think anyone in the room at that moment took a single breath.

The last part of the walk-though was the kitchen. As I entered the rather small kitchen, my heart began to race with anxiety. When I looked over at Beckah, she too seemed to feel the anxiety and mentioned feelings of wanting to pace around the kitchen.

This view shows the path the murderer took through the apartment with the victim's body... he dragged her out of the bedroom, through the living room, and into the kitchen.

"He used to do his thinking in this room...he also used to pace a lot here," Beckah said.

As I continued to film Beckah, she looked at me with a rather serious look on her face. I asked if she needed a moment to gather herself and then pressed the pause button on the video camera to find out what was wrong. Then Beckah leaned close to my face.

"Katie, this question is directed to you by the murder victim," Beckah said. "Just tell the family where the head is."

Beckah began crying profusely. I just stood there with Beckah and the clients looking at me, waiting for an answer.

My mouth dropped open and I became pale in the face. "Yes," I slowly said back. For many years I worked at a State Prison for men and this comment was the exact words I spoke to the inmate who was sentenced for a brutal murder of a woman; he had stabbed her repeatedly and then dismembered her body and threw the remains away in different outside locations. When Beckah asked me that certain question, it was as if the spirit of the murdered woman began to heal. She needed someone to

This is the kitchen where the woman's body was cut into pieces before being disposed of.

acknowledge her death and, because the information was not clicking for me, she felt the need to use the phrase to jog my memory so that I would recognize the case.

The Conclusion....

After regrouping ourselves from the drama in the kitchen, we decided to use some of our paranormal equipment and interact with both female spirits. The bedroom was where most of the activity was happening, so we decided to try that location first.

Beckah sat on the edge of the client's bed and began using the dowsing rods, asking questions. "If a murder took place in this room, please cross the wands?" Right away, the dowsing wands crossed.

Both female spirits interacted through the dowsing wands and answered every question Beckah asked. I stood off to the side during this part and filmed. Even though Beckah gave the clients full details about the murder and the Victorian era woman, it is also great to get the spirits communicating with the paranormal equipment. Every step during an investigation should be documented and recorded using both analog and digital voice recorders, as well as video recorders. That way you have every moment on tape. It is also helpful as recording devices

The bedroom... This corner was where the clients said they often saw a dark female figure.

will gather EVPs (electronic voice phenomena) and when you're writing your findings because the parts you may not remember are clearly recorded on tape.

Beckah asked if the clients and I could step out of the bedroom for a few minutes while she helped the female murder victim cross over. We all agreed and waited in the living room. After the investigation was completed, we sat down with the clients to answer any questions and help them to process the information. The clients seemed more relaxed. After some time spent talking, Beckah and I left.

A few days passed and I thought it would be good to check in with the young couple. They did not experience any paranormal activity the night of the investigation and had not still. The young woman has been sleeping through the night. Unfortunately, they will be moving out of the apartment soon due to the horrifying history behind their apartment. While reviewing the evidence that night — I just could not wait until the next day — I found that we did capture a few EVPs of the murdered woman moaning in agony on the voice recorders.

~~~~~

HANG MAN

A young man had contacted me about some paranormal experiences his girlfriend and her roommate had been having. Apparently, it was getting so bad that both of the women would not sleep in the rented townhouse. He did not explain much to me over the phone and thought it would be better to talk with his girlfriend in person. I agreed and again had brought Beckah along with me for the investigation. It was nighttime when we traveled to the location of the supposed haunting and, as I drove into the driveway, a sudden downpour of rain started. Beckah stayed in the vehicle until I was done interviewing the client and her boyfriend.

The woman was in her early thirties and not on any medication. I asked my usual questions about her experiences, including "Where is most of the activity occurring?" The woman explained that while both she and the roommate are sleeping in separate rooms, they see an outline of a man standing at the foot of the bed. Sometimes the bed shakes, and then footsteps walking upstairs into the large attic can be heard. Now the attic door is on the same floor as the women's bedrooms. The second floor is where most of the activity takes place and is where the attic door is also located. The whole time I was talking with the client and her boyfriend downstairs in the living room, footsteps could be heard above us. Someone was defiantly walking around in the attic...for the attic stairs are right above the living room and no one was upstairs at that time. The woman talked about being pushed while in the bathroom and how the shampoo bottles in the shower upstairs are thrown at her. I thought it might be a good time to call Beckah in, so she could start her walk-though of the home.

The Man....

Right away Beckah said, "There is a man here — and he is pissed!"

My eyes tried not to show concern because the client was standing right next to me and she was scared to death as it was. I showed Beckah the downstairs living room and she did not pick up on anything negative in the room.

"We need to go up," she said.

All four of us headed upstairs and Beckah was drawn to the bathroom right away. She stated that the male spirit did not like the fact women lived in *his* house and hated the woman's female products in *his* bathroom. The air was not heavy like in some spirit haunting cases, but a feeling of unease could be felt while standing in the bathroom.

Beckah stood in the hallway for a moment and stated that this male spirit watches the client sleeping at night. Beckah talked about how the spirit likes to terrorize the women who live here by sometimes moving or shaking the bed while they are sleeping. Beckah quietly mentioned to me that this spirit is very negative and will have to be "forced" (having a loved one who has passed assist with the escort of the unwilling spirit to cross over) to leave and cross over to the other side.

We then continued to the attic. As I opened the attic door, a rush of cold air hit my face. I took a step backwards and decided to continue up the attic's old wooden stairs. The attic was old and seemed to have the original wooden beams and floor. Even the windows looked original to the home. Beckah walked around and stated that the male spirit spends most of his time there in the attic pacing back and forth across the floor.

"He was losing everything and just could not cope," Beckah said.

Apparently, while this male spirit was still living, he had made some bad business decisions and lost most of his money. His wife tried to stick by him, but he could not deal with her disappointment and thought it would be better if she was without him. He had been in and out of depression for a long period before especially when his business began to suffer.

"He was into textiles," Beckah said. "I feel like something happened…I want to say it was an accident or something natural, maybe a flood or fire. People died and I just don't feel like he was able to completely recover his business after that. He was not used to feeling like a failure. He does not fail!"

The lines in Beckah's face turned harsh at that moment — the determination and anger she was picking up off the spirit were evident in her countenance. She took a deep breath and continued her reading.

As I was walking around the attic taking pictures, Beckah pointed to an old wooden beam above her head. "He hanged himself on this beam and is blaming every woman who moves into this house for his misfortune," she said, looking up at the old beam.

This is the beam where Beckah indicated that the spirit had hanged himself.

Katie's Experience....

At this point, I decided to have the client and Beckah investigate more in the bathroom, and I would spend some time up in the attic with no lights on. I made sure that I was armed with a video camcorder and a small flashlight.

Walking slowly around the attic, I decided to talk to the male spirit and ask him to make his presence known to me or on the video camcorder. Just after asking the spirit to do this, a felt the sensation of someone breathing on my neck. I continued talk to the spirit as I walked more around the attic. Again, I felt the breathing and the feeling of someone stepping on the heel of my shoe. Yet the most exciting part of the investigation was hearing footsteps following me around the attic. To make sure the footsteps were not coming from the old floorboards, I went in every corner and tested the floor.

I then tested the floorboards in the middle of the attic. Now, with these types of old wooden floorboards, sometimes there are in fact loose boards, which make it sound like someone was walking behind the individual. I could not find any logical answer for the footsteps other than perhaps this in fact could be the result of the male spirit. Once I gathered my information, I headed out of the attic and down to the second floor. I filled the client and Beckah in on the experiences I encountered while up in the attic.

As this view shows, there was possible spirit activity taking place when I was in the attic by myself trying to contact the spirit.

The Conclusion....

Beckah came across no paranormal activity in the bathroom and decided it was a good time to help this spirit cross over. This process took a few extra moments as Beckah needed to call her grandfather (who had passed when Beckah was very little) in to help escort the unwilling spirit over to the other side.

"For the most part, the male spirit was scared to cross over and was afraid he would be badly judged. He then became grounded," Beckah said.

The investigation was over and both Beckah and I spent a few more moments talking with the client and her boyfriend. She still did not want to spend the night in her bedroom even though the spirit was now gone. We told the client to try to relax for the rest of the night and call us if she had any questions or issues. We were driving down the street, heading home, when the cell phone rang. It was the client again. She swore the male spirit was still in the attic and could *hear* the footsteps. We reassured her that the male spirit was not still in the home, nor was any other spirit. This was residual energy left over from the clearing and that in a day or two it would disappear. She did not believe me and spent the next few days at her boyfriend's apartment. Honestly, if I did not work in the paranormal field, I would do the same thing.

After a few days passed, so did the feeling of the haunting. There has been no activity to date and the client is spending the nights in her own home now. While reviewing the evidence from the case, I did catch possible spirit activity on camera film.

CRYING... "BOOGEYMAN"

This case was brought to me by another paranormal research group that felt after investigating this particular client's home it was not haunted. Nevertheless, the client was insistent on getting another opinion. The client felt that the previous paranormal group was no help whatsoever and so, exasperated, they referred her to me. It seemed that the woman lived a few towns over from me, and the paranormal group (they were located in another state) asked if I could visit and talk with the client in person.

The client and I scheduled a date to come to her home only a couple of days away. She was relieved when she heard me say I could help her. I asked the previous paranormal group for their opinion on the case; they gave me a little forewarning, saying the woman had about six kids and a boyfriend who spent weeks at a time living at the client's home. They reiterated that they had not gotten any physical evidence and that they had not actually talked to the kids because the investigators only wanted one person in the home. The reason for this request is simple — the less people there, the more you can control the environment.

I spoke to the case manager for the group and she told me that the mother (we will call her Brenda) did not actually experience a lot on her own. The activity seemed to revolve around her children, with the eldest daughter (we will call her Maggie) seemingly a particular focus for the spirit activity. The paranormal group as a whole was completely unconvinced and believed that there may be some medical or psychological trauma or issues associated with the victims in this case. Maggie, it seemed, suffered the worst out of all of the family members; she would pass out without notice and then quickly regain consciousness. This only happened when she was in the house.

While talking to investigators, Brenda also said that one day she had come home from work and there was a kitchen knife in one of her surround sound speakers in the living room. When she asked the kids what happened, they told her an elaborate story about how they were all playing in the living room and Maggie was standing near the speaker talking with a younger sibling. As the kids happily played their games, all of a sudden Maggie screamed — a knife catapulted through the air and the blade stabbed into the speaker! I had not yet met the family myself, so I could form no firm conclusions. I thanked the paranormal group for their effort and promised to keep them informed. I could not wait to find out what exactly was going on in the apartment.

It was dark when I arrived, but I was still about a half hour early. Beckah joined me on this investigation just in case there were any spirits that needed help. She also has a way with getting information out of otherwise hesitant families that is needed to further understand the phenomena. As an investigator, I try to be as objective as possible when walking into a client's home. However, the information that the other paranormal group had given me was lingering. As a corrections officer, one of the best tools I learned was how to ask the same question in a thousand different ways to be sure that the stories are consistent. I intended on using that technique tonight; when a victim goes through a traumatic experience, things are remembered in clear detail. No matter how many times they are asked, their story should never change. If it does, it is a clear indication that he or she may be lying or exaggerating the truth. Either way, I needed to know.

We sat outside of the apartment building for a couple of minutes figuring out our strategy. Beckah would talk to the mom while I talked to Maggie and then we would take a moment to step out and compare information. With our plan firmly in mind, we knocked on the door and...walked into chaos. I do not think I had realized until that moment just how cramped a three-bedroom apartment could be. Five of the kids were getting ready to go sleep over the boyfriend's house, though the couple had been together for so long that the kids often referred to him as their "stepdad." Ranging in ages from four to thirteen, it was a madhouse. Brenda asked us to take a seat while she and her boyfriend got the kids finished and ready to go.

Haunted or Attention-Seeker....

We waited patiently amid the chaos of flying clothes and kids scrambling from one room to the other. From where we sat, we saw directly into one of the kid's bedrooms where Maggie was helping her little brother get his clothes together. Then all of a sudden, we heard a loud thud. Everyone ran to the room; Brenda got there before anyone else — she was on the floor with Maggie who lay there unconscious. "Maggie! Maggie!" Brenda yelled.

All of a sudden, the young girl came to. Beckah and Brenda helped Maggie get up and to the couch. I noticed something then...Maggie seemed to be smiling under her mother's attentive gaze. I knew that the real inquiry would have to wait until the other kids left, so I decided not to pursue that angle until after the investigation. Finally, the kids were out the door with their "stepfather" and only Brenda and Maggie remained. Beckah took Brenda upstairs while I stayed downstairs with Maggie.

Brenda XXXX Interview, 1/27/2007

The following was taken from original case transcript, though I have taken the liberty of removing some of the more personal parts of the conversations, leaving those most pertinent to the case.

Beckah: When did you begin noticing the paranormal activity?

Brenda: Well I grew up in a home that was haunted. We moved into this house about six months ago. It was about two months in when Maggie started having issues and from there everything went downhill.

Beckah: What is your religious belief system?

Brenda: Earth worship. I've been getting more into my Native American side. Rediscovering it really. My mama was into it. This situation has caused me to find my faith again.

Beckah: Are you or Maggie on any medications? I saw her faint earlier — is that common and, if it is, has a doctor seen her?

Brenda: It has become more common in the last month or so. No, neither of us is on any type of prescription medications. (sighs) Maggie has been to see the doctor; they…ah, they told us that it was most likely stress. I don't believe that though, I mean I guess it could be.

Beckah: Does she ever say she feels sick or upset right before fainting?

Brenda: No, no, she doesn't. She will be right in the middle of talking and boom! She is down and out.

Beckah: Okay… Otherwise, they found her to be completely healthy.

Brenda: Yep, which frustrated me like hell. There is more too; the other kids have seen things as well.

Beckah: Has it always been centered on Maggie?

Brenda: Yeah, it has. When the kids see things, it's around Maggie. Like the time that they saw a cup crash into the wall that separates the kitchen from the living room.

Beckah: Did they see the cup fly?

Brenda: Well, no, they were playing with the Xbox. They heard the crash and saw Maggie standing there with the cup in pieces. She said something threw it at her.

Beckah: Mmmhmmm… Okay, so what you are telling me is that you have never physically experienced anything, but that Maggie does all of the time?

Brenda: No, no. I have experienced things. I've seen shadows, especially in the bedroom downstairs where Maggie…well, you know, where she passed out. I could see the shadow and these beady red eyes looking at me. It just gave me the creeps.

Beckah: Where were you at this time?

Brenda: I was on the couch watching TV. It's right next to the doorway, so it's easy to peer in there.

Beckah: Were you fully awake or starting to doze?

Brenda: I had been dozing on and off all evening. I had to work a double and my body was tired, but my mind was very much awake. Sometimes it helps me to conk out in front of the television.

Beckah: Alright then… I think I've heard enough.

Maggie XXXX Interview, 1/27/2007

> While Brenda was so open about her own experiences with Beckah, downstairs Maggie's interview was not quite as simple. Here is a part of the transcript just to give you an idea.

Katie: How are you feeling?
Maggie: Fine.
Katie: Just fine? Maggie, you just fainted not ten minutes ago.
Maggie: Yeah.
Katie: Well, doesn't your head hurt or anything? Do you feel funny at all?
Maggie: No
Katie: How often does this happen, Maggie?
Maggie: I dunno.
Katie: What is it like living with such a big family?
Maggie: It's alright, I guess.

Katie: Maggie, how old are you?

Maggie: Fourteen

Katie: Wow, that's a tough age. Are you and your mom close?

Maggie: Kinda…Like you said we have a big family.

Katie: Where is your dad?

Maggie: They got a divorce…he moved down to Virginia.

Katie: How long ago did that happen?

Maggie: Last year

Katie: Do you feel that you get enough attention, Maggie?

Maggie: No. My mom is really busy…we don't talk a lot.

Katie: Do you sometimes feel like you should get more?

Maggie: I dunno. I do a lot around the house.

Katie: Maggie, do you ever feel anything before you faint? A funny feeling in your stomach, or dizzy?

Maggie: A little dizzy sometimes.

Katie: Talk to me about the cup that flew at you. What happened earlier that day?

Maggie: (exhales loudly) Nothing.

Katie: That doesn't sound like a nothing answer. Did something upset you the day the cup broke?

Maggie: My brother wouldn't let me play on the Xbox, even though mom said I could have an hour before she left. Then I called her and she just said let my brothers have it and that I could get it after they went to bed. But I had school in the morning and I wasn't supposed to be able to stay up. Not that I'm complaining. It's just that I really wanted to play and instead, they got what they wanted.

Katie: Wow…it sounds like you have some anger in you. Tell me about the knife, Maggie. Was that a bad day too?

Maggie: Yeah, I had to watch my brothers and sisters that night too. Mom went out for a little while. I wanted to go over my friend Aisha's house that day, but instead I had to watch them.

Katie: Sounds like you take care of your siblings a lot.

Maggie: Yeah, but (older sister) doesn't have to. She does a lot of things at school and Mom says she has to focus.

Katie: Do you believe that a cup can fly through the air?

Maggie: Yes, it did.
Katie: But no one else saw it Maggie.
Maggie: (whining) Yeah I know, but it did.
Katie: Okay. It did happen.

Soon after this, I had finished the interview and asked to speak with Beckah outside. We compared our findings and found three things to be the most common variables. Firstly, Maggie; secondly, none of the physical activity happened when the parents were home; and thirdly, all of the physical phenomena happened when no one was looking. For example, the breaking cup… everyone was looking at the television in the living room, not in the kitchen, and Maggie and her mother's own testimony places her there alone. Maggie admitted she would like to have a little extra attention and that she has a lot of stress in her life taking care of the younger siblings while mom is at work.

The Investigation….

We decided against meeting with both of them until after the investigation when we saw what evidence we could drum up. We asked Brenda if Maggie would not mind going to her friend's house a couple of apartments down. We wanted to see what type of evidence we would get without Maggie being there and then again when she was.

We had Brenda sit in with us. We called out for bangs and knocks while in the living room. I have learned over years that you do not antagonize in order to gain evidence. If any is to be found, it will present itself. Patience is key, so we waited. Beckah had the voice recorder and was asking the spirit about his or her life and death.

Nothing really happened that could not be explained. We heard footsteps upstairs at one point; it sounded like a child running. We went to the neighbor's house on the right side of Brenda's apartment and asked if they had kids. They said they had two boys; I asked if they were running around a couple of seconds ago and she said they had just been sent upstairs to get ready for bed. I sent

Beckah back to the apartment and asked the neighbor if she could have one or both of the kids run back up and down the stairs. I had my walkie-talkie with me and so did Beckah. The mother did as I asked and the two boys came storming down the stairs and back up. Beckah asked if that was us in the walkie-talkie.

After another couple of hours of sitting and calling out, we decided to have Maggie come join us. At first, she seemed nervous. Beckah explained how we were going to do an experiment. She talked about how we had noticed that no one ever saw anything, so we were going to go in the kitchen with her and form a wide circle around her. We wanted her to get into that same angry state she was in before; we would all close our eyes. We formed a circle large enough to give her room, but tight enough so that she could not access cabinets or get out from between us. We asked Maggie to think about everything that was unfair, everything that made her feel anger, and to bring it up to a boiling point. You could see the changes in emotion overcome her face. When we finally felt she was in the right place, we began the experiment.

Nothing happened. We asked her to call out for it…nothing. Therefore, we decided to take a different approach. We tried one last experiment. This would prove it. Earlier, while setting up our equipment, we had put some cameras around the house that were recording video to a tape. The cameras were wireless and on the small side. We had an idea of what may have been going on prior to setup (after Maggie left) and so we thought maybe Maggie had not caught on to the fact that she was being videotaped.

We told Maggie we were going to leave her alone in the kitchen. Beckah reassured her that she was protected and that nothing would harm her. Beckah set up a psychic shield for Maggie using a technique called Bubbling Up. It puts the object or person in a balloon of protective psychic energy. We gave her the audio recorder and walkie-talkie and explained we would be right outside to call on the radio.

After ten to fifteen minutes, we heard her shaky voice on the radio. "C-can you guys come in please?" We came in and what we saw absolutely amazed us. The kitchen table was in shambles:

papers that were previously on it were strewn about the floor, one of the kitchen cupboards was open, and two of the plates had smashed on the floor, along with a clock that hung on the wall. In the living room, a blanket that had covered the couch was thrown across the television hanging haphazardly.

"Wow," I said. I do not think there was anything else to say. It seemed that Maggie had escaped harm. Brenda decided immediately that they were going to sleep over her boyfriend's house. I figured we had stressed out the two women enough for the night. We helped them clean up and then gathered our gear and left.

The Conclusion....

A couple of days later, I got a frantic call from Brenda. I was actually happy to hear from her because Beckah and I had reviewed the evidence and had some interesting things to share with her. She told us, "The house is torn apart. I do not know what happened. I came home from work. Everyone was asleep and things were all jumbled up." I told her not to worry; Beckah and I were on our way over and that we had some things to share with her as well.

We were at her house three hours later with laptop and videotape in hand. When we walked in, we realized she really was not kidding; it looked like a tornado had run through the house. Nevertheless, Beckah and I were firm in our knowledge of the culprit. We sat down with Brenda... Maggie wanted to be there, but we thought it better that she go to her "stepfather's" house with the other kids. First, we played a portion of the audio recorder... not to hear something we recorded, but rather something that was not recorded. At the end of the tape, you hear a soft girl's voice saying, "How," and then the tape goes blank. None of the time the phenomenon was taking place was recorded. As soon as we left, you hear the female voice and then the tape recorder is shut off.

We asked if we could use her video player. We went past the unimportant parts, getting to the end. We had placed a camera in the tiny hall that led to the laundry room. It gave a full view of the kitchen, but was an inconspicuous spot. From that angle, you could see Maggie in the kitchen — and we watched her shut off the recorder. The rest made Brenda's face blanch and her mouth dropped as she watched her daughter destroy her kitchen.

I then talked to her about Maggie's need for attention, and asked that Maggie be brought back. When Maggie finally got there, we showed her the tape. Anger and guilt consumed her...anger at being caught and guilt for lying. Beckah then helped mother and daughter open up a dialogue about their feelings and needs. Brenda agreed to try to be home more often; Maggie agreed to be more patient with her siblings. Since that time, Brenda and Maggie's relationship, although not perfect, has improved greatly and there has been no other "paranormal" activity. However, they did discover that Maggie's bouts of fainting were due to a condition called Vasovagal Syncope. Also called the "common faint," in Maggie case, it was related to stress and a mild case of hypoglycemia.

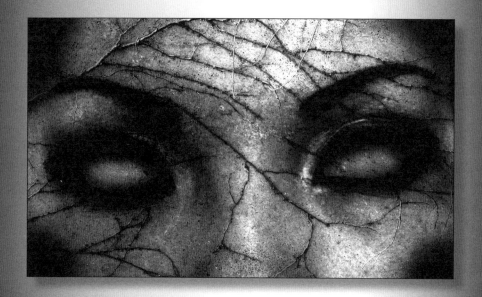

Chapter Five:
ALIEN ENCOUNTERS

Out from the closets at night these entities occasionally appear, closer and closer to us as we lay in our beds, paralyzed by some unseen force. Sometimes a bright, blazing light comes down and shines through our bedroom windows or closet doors and *they're* standing before their next victim with only a blank stare upon their faces and suddenly...*we vanish until morning*.

Many of today's society see this as a new thing, at least only since the Roswell incident in the 1950s. However, let me just say it goes back a lot further than that. Not just one hundred, two hundred, or three hundred years — it goes all the way back to the time of the Mayans, Sumerian, and biblical times. Erich Von Daniken, who I find fascinating, and others like him who believe in the Ancient Astronauts have created a compelling argument for alien encounters in primitive history. Here is an excerpt from the *Book of Enoch*; this man, Enoch, was very open with his spiritual experiences including those that many now suspect were actually abductions.

"And appeared to me two men very tall such as I have never on earth
And their faces shone like the sun and eyes were like burning lamps and fire came forth their lips
Their dress had the appearance of feathers feet were purple their wings were brighter than gold their hands whiter than snow

They stood at the head of bed and called me by my name I awoke from my and saw clearly these men standing in front of me I hastened and made obeisance to them and was terrified the appearance of my countenance was changed from

And these men said to me "Be of good cheer be not afraid the everlasting God hath sent us to and lo to day thou shalt ascend with us into heaven"

[Of the taking up of Enoch, how the Angels took him up into the first heaven]

"It came to pass when I had spoken to my sons these men summoned me and took me on their wings and placed me on the clouds

And lo the clouds moved

And again going higher I saw the air and going still higher I saw the ether and they placed me in the first heaven

And they showed me a very great sea greater than the earthly sea

Of the Angels who rule the Stars

And they brought before my face the elders and the rulers of the orders of the stars and they showed me the two hundred angels who rule the stars and their heavenly service."

~ *The Book of the Secrets of Enoch*, 1896

The Boogeyman or An Alien?

Some folks swear it is the "boogeyman" that takes them at night while others claim it is an entity called "Grey." The "grey" alien seems to be the most commonly seen by those individuals who claimed to have been abducted; this entity is described as being rather short with a head much larger than a human's in size and large black slanted eyes, which seem to have a kind of lens protecting them. Many abductees say the eyes bring a soothing feeling when you look into them.

The entity also has two small nostril holes and a small slit for a mouth, but does not open to communicate. Instead, communication is through what is called "telepathy," which is a process of psychic

Is it an alien? Boogeyman? Or something else entirely?

communication using their extra sensory perception to transmit thoughts between each other and the victim. The body structure seems to be small and rather thin, with long thin arms that stretch to the knees and thin legs that have no apparent markings. What isn't known is why they come to visit us. What is the reason behind their late night visits? Some researchers claim that the human race is being studied and strange medical experiments are being performed on the abductees' bodies. The events that transpired are then erased or suppressed from their memories and the abductees are returned home.

Since the famous abduction cases of "Antonio Villas Boas" in 1957 and "The Betty and Barney Hill" case in 1961, more people are coming forward and claiming to have been abducted by these entities. Betty and Barney Hill were abducted from a vehicle, not a bedroom, and Antonio Villas Boas was out plowing in his fields at night to avoid the hot sun, but what about the nightly visits from these entities that involve the bedroom? How often is it that aliens really make their presence known there? There is at least one infamous case of a boogeyman-type alien that came and snatched a person from his bedroom and that case is the one of a man named Whitley Strieber....

The Whitley Strieber Story

It is not uncommon for an alien abductee to be alone during their experience, although there are plenty of cases where multiple people are abducted at the same time. With Whitley, it was an individual experience, but he was not alone during the abduction. He grew up with a wonderful imagination, both powerful and intense. Prior to the actual abduction, Whitley was at the time already a well-known author of horror and fantasy books. Two of them — *Wolfen* (1978) and *The Hunger* (1981) — had actually been made into movies in the 1980s. With a great following and riding high with his success, he and his family decided to vacation at their cabin in Upper State New York over the Christmas holiday in 1985. Whitley always had an eye towards security and safety, so he had only recently had a top-of-the-line security system installed.

It was the day after Christmas, December 26, 1985 at 11 p.m. when he set his security system. He and his family then went to bed for the evening, but he awoke a couple of hours later after hearing an odd noise. He felt as though someone was in the house or something had happened. What met his eyes when he opened them was definitely not what he expected. One of the "grey" beings stood before him... That is the last thing he remembered until he found himself sitting in the woods surrounding his cabin.

After the incident, memories came in pieces to him, like that of a large eyed owl in the window. He also claimed that he had been to see the doctor because he was not feeling well immediately after the experience; he became irritable and just felt completely off-center, so he began to really investigate. Whitley recalled that when he picked up his first UFO book, just holding it filled him with a sense of dread. Ultimately, he and his family decided that hypnosis might be the best and only option for regaining the memories he lost during the event.

Hypnosis is still a highly debated concept within the paranormal community. Yes, it does work, but only for those who are open to it. People have manipulated hypnosis sessions before, using them to establish rapes that never happened and abductions that were nothing more than a dream. Personally, I see hypnosis as a great tool when used under the right conditions...as did Whitley and his family. They all decided to undergo hypnosis. Whitley described his skepticism and his eventual meeting with the psychiatrist in an article he wrote for *MUFON UFO* newsmagazine in December 1986.

"Before this experience, I was not only disinterested in the UFO phenomenon, I must admit that I was pretty much of a skeptic. I really hadn't thought about the question in years. I thought that the matter was extremely unimportant and that the people who reported seeing objects were simply making mistakes. I was not aware of abduction accounts at all, and it took weeks for me to connect what had happened to me to the idea of a nonhuman presence. The connection was made because — by a fortuitous circumstance – my brother sent me a book for Christmas called *Sciences and the UFOs*. At the end of this book they described a 'typical abduction experience.' To my acute embarrassment, I realized that this was very similar to what had happened to me. Budd Hopkins' name was mentioned in the book, and after an agonizing period of soul-searching, I telephoned him. He in turn put me in touch with Dr. Donald Klein, Chairman of the New York State Department of Psychiatry, who became my therapist and hypnotist."

When you undergo regressive hypnosis to uncover locked memories, an individual is able to remember them even when out of the hypnotic state. What the Strieber family remembered was equally disturbing and intriguing.

During his session, Whitley remembered being lifted off of his bed by an unseen force, almost as though he were floating, and then taken into a UFO aircraft. He identified three different species of aliens: one was almost robot like and small in stature; the second was short and stocky; the third was very wispy looking, thin and frail, with eyes similar to black buttons. The other two, though, had the slanted eyes that have become the hallmark of the UFO alien.

Whitley believed that medical procedures had taken place while he was there and in fact claimed that they had inserted a needle into his brain. During another part of the session, he talks about how they actually inserted a piece of their equipment into his rectum and took a blood sample by making an incision in his finger. He also discovered that he had been having abduction experiences ever since he was very young.

Whitley's wife, Anne, found that she had often witnessed UFO activity around others and his son Andrew said during hypnosis that he remembered a weird dream he had where there were a bunch of little doctors and they took him from his bed and put him on a cot outside on the porch. He was scared, but he remembered hearing them say "We won't hurt you" repeatedly in his mind.

Later, Whitley talked about his anal probe experience in an interview in 2005 with www.Karmapolis.be. The interviewer, who went by the name of Karmatoo, asked many questions of the infamous abductee, varying from how and if you can prevent alien abductions to his opinion on the series "Taken" (which just in case you are curious Whitley describes as completely false and inaccurate). However, what caught my attention was Whitley's openness about his experience with the medical tests and examinations they performed on him.

In the interview, Karmatoo asked Whitley, "Some people refer to the aliens as 'intruders'; you call them 'visitors'. Why?" W. S. replied:

Because I don't think it's time to make a decision about this. "Intruders" says that we know something about their motives; "visitors" simply that they are here. On the night of December 26, 1985, I was raped with a device commonly used in animal husbandry called an electrostimulator. This device is inserted into the rectum and conducts a small electrical current into the area of the prostate that causes erection and ejaculation. My ejaculate was taken. I was badly injured and my doctor felt on examining me that I had been raped. Obviously, I was attacked by "intruders." But why? If we were desperate to save the human species and needed genetic material from a species on another world who, we feared, would not understand our need and would resist giving it to us, we would not only take it, we would feel morally justified in doing so.

After this initial rough encounter, I spent eleven years in the most complex possible relationship with the visitors and many people connected with them. I have written only a little about this, because I decided that the culture was not ready for my story, given that I was attacked on so many different levels, misrepresented, lied about by U.S. government agents, and laughed at. The "rectal probe" became a cliché of modern humor. I do not feel that this cultural reaction was appropriate or useful, and I have therefore kept most of my experience, and in particular the powers I have gained, to myself, and will continue to do so.

Almost all of his experiences began with him in his bedroom paralyzed.

Having been in the paranormal field for over twenty years, and especially during the writing of this book, I have come to realize there are many conditions that can simulate this experience, including sleep paralysis. As we discussed earlier, it can be accompanied by both auditory and visual hallucinations.

After over a dozen hypnosis sessions, Dr. Klein decided to pose the theory that maybe Whitley was suffering from temporal lobe epilepsy (TLE). Whitley was very open to the idea and underwent the necessary tests to see if he in fact suffered from some form of epileptic seizures. The results came back clean, but one thing I have learned in my studies is that TLE is difficult to catch. Look at the following section and draw your own conclusions: alien abduction, sleep paralysis, TLE, or just an overactive imagination?

Either way, it has paid off for Strieber: his book *Communion*, which relates the experiences he remembers having while under hypnosis, hit the *New York Times* bestseller list and stayed there for multiple weeks. He sold over two million copies of his paperback and 300,000 of the hardcover. He has also followed *Communion* with a succession of other abduction related books and, over time, some people have noticed changes in his story.

For example, in *Communion* and *Breakthrough: The Next Step*, Whitley discusses in the first book how he read about (physicist) Dr. Sarbacher and wanted to interview him and was unable to because the man died in July 1986, a few days before Whitley became aware of a letter Dr. Sarbacher had written and peaked Strieber's interest in him. However, in 1997, Whitley wrote *Breakthrough* and again talked about his initial awareness of Dr. Sarbacher. Only this time, instead of saying the doctor died, Whitley talks about how he set up an interview with the man and that he first read Sarbacher's letter in August 1986. However, in *Communion*, did not Sarbacher die in July of that year? Hmmmm... questions, questions.

Temporal Lobe Epilepsy

There are many different forms of seizures, each involving or encompassing different aspects of the brain. This form of epilepsy is the most common cause of partial seizures — the person is having an epileptic episode, but is still aware of their environment. Epileptic seizures typically show signs before they begin. These warnings are called "auras," the odd emotional or physical feeling that you get just before an epileptic episode. They can range from changes in bodily sensations (particularly in the stomach area) to changes in your familiar environment (things seem more "real" and "alive") and can also be accompanied by a feeling of extreme fear or déjà vu.

The first researcher to document the connection between paranormal experiences and temporal lobe epilepsy was Norman Geschwind. He recognized a set of symptoms typical to the episodes aside from the auras. These included Hyperreligiosity, a toxic and powerful addiction to religion and faith. Oftentimes this is not in fact a need to join Buddhism for instance, but rather more destructive doom and gloom cults. One perfect example of this is Marshall Applewhite, who led the Heaven's Gate cult to suicide; he also believed he was a UFO abductee and later formed the essential practices and rituals of the cult.

Another symptom is hypergraphia, which is an overwhelming urge to write; both Van Gogh and Lewis Carroll were believed to suffer from hypergraphia. Lewis Carroll in particular wrote over 98,000 letters in varying ways, including rubes, backwards, and in circular patterns.

Geschwind also found that fainting spells could be directly connected to temporal lobe epilepsy as well as pedantism, which is someone who is overly concerned with rules and details. They are obsessed with precision and make a show of their learning. Obsessive Compulsive Disorder actually has a base in pedantism in that the person with the disorder actually becomes obsessed with the rules they have made for themselves or those that are malformations of actual laws and formalities.

Neurotheologians assert that many of those suffering from TLE have a natural aptitude for connecting to the spiritual authorities. They believe that those who suffered with this form of epilepsy in the past actually took positions as shamans and other religious figures. Some causes of TLE are:

† Previous infections, such as meningitis and encephalitis, and abnormal patterns of electrical activity in the brain.

† Also, lesions, genetic syndromes, and traumatic injuries.

† Seizures can actually be one of the first indications of a brain tumor.

† AVM (arteriovenous malformation), which is a blood vessel disorder, and others like it can also be the cause of seizures.

Here are two examples of Lewis Carroll's many letters. One was written in a circular pattern; the other backwards. *Courtesy of philobiblon. com.*

Other common symptoms of TLE are:

† Hallucinations of all kinds and that include all five senses.
† Forced turning of the eyes.
† Nausea and rapid heartbeat or pulse.
† Changes in speak, personality, awareness, thought, and vision.

It is believed that most who suffer from TLE will never have a full-blown seizure. However, there are documented instances where individuals diagnosed with this form of epilepsy do in fact suffer full-blown episodes and temporal lobe epilepsy can be such a debilitating illness for those who do have this disorder. For some surgery may be the only option, although there are medications out there that can help control the seizures, but the treatment may not work for everyone. The surgery removes the abnormal tissue in the brain, which is causing the odd electrical activity in the brain. Many psychologists and medical professionals, who meet with individuals who believe they have been abducted, claim that is some form of TLE manifesting itself.

This is not my area of expertise; I am not a professional psychologist, doctor, or ufologist, so I cannot purport any true knowledge of TLE except for that which I have garnered from the medical and UFO community. Although I personally cannot at this point believe that all abduction experiences are in fact some form of temporal lobe dysfunction; I have dealt with abductee cases during my years of paranormal exploration and, from those interviews and investigations, there were one or two cases that just could not convince me it was due to a mental imbalance or physiological disorder. Read on....

BRiGHT LiGHTS

A woman had contacted me some time ago with an issue she was having with strange lights that seemed to be following her. Now, as I stated earlier, I am not a professional ufologist, but I am familiar with the basics of alien abduction and contact experiences. Connie is a married mother of three young children and was in a state of real distress when I met her. At first, she started talking about maybe it was a paranormal issue, but eventually she began to talk about her own experiences, which totally turned the tables for me. I was expecting a spirit haunting or even perhaps a demonic haunting. What I got was a first-hand report of multiple alien encounters. Connie was originally from Lewiston, Maine, but had moved to Exeter, New Hampshire, in the early 1990s. The town of Exeter is considered New England's Roswell by many UFO researchers, so I was not surprised to hear that her story started in this area. Thoughts flooded my mind: could this woman truly be experiencing some form of alien contact? My ears needed to hear more of the story to make any type of conclusion.

I have always believed that we humans cannot be the only intelligent life out there in the universe and beyond. There are many shows like "The X-Files" and "UFO Hunters" that give us a glimpse of just what might be out there, perhaps even watching us. Oftentimes I will scour the Internet for new cases about UFOs and I have always found MUFON (Mutual UFO Network) a plethora of resources, articles, and information regarding both the skeptical and die-hard believers' viewpoints and investigations. So, if I personally could not help Connie, at least I could point her in the right direction.

Because of my years working in the paranormal field, I am inherently skeptical. You have to be...otherwise, the results of any investigation would be considered essentially null and void. If a person looks at something with a decision already made, well then you will find a way to make it fit your pre-conceived notions, which can, in some cases, be detrimental to the client, especially if they are in fact suffering from a medical or psychological condition. So my mind was open to listening, as I thought this would be a rather interesting conversation. However, what the woman shared with me proved to be compelling evidence that just maybe we are not alone in the universe.

Connie was in her mid-forties and of a petite build. She looked a little stressed and tired. The first thing we went through was her medical history; she said that she had been healthy all of her life, but that she had in her teens had been on anti-depression medication for a short time. Her parents were divorcing and, as any teenager would, she found it hard to deal with; she was on the medication for a year and a half. She met her future husband at the age of twenty-two and from then on Connie said her life had felt completely blessed. She indicated that since the abductions began, things had started to deteriorate in their relationship. Her husband did not believe her experiences and this built resentment between them. Connie felt she could not talk to friends or family about this issue and feared no one would understand. Therefore, she decided to search for help within the paranormal community for answers.

Connie began to talk about the first time she experienced the UFO encounter — it was Tuesday, October 16, 2001 around 5:30 in the morning. She always had been a fussy dresser and had gone through multiple items of clothing prior to actually figuring out what to wear. While she was cleaning up her mess, she saw these bright flashing lights outside her bedroom window. Connie explained how she had Venetian blinds and they were closed, so all she saw was a strobe like light flashing repeatedly in multiple colors of red, green, blue, white, and yellow. Not quite sure what it was, she went to the window, but as she went to pull up the blind, she heard a loud booming noise. When she finally got the blind up, the lights and whatever was flashing them were gone. This not only affected her, but her children woke up because of the noise. Her husband worked third shift and so he was not home yet. Although she was worried about it, her mind began to form explanations. By the time her husband got home, her mind was onto other things, like getting the kids to school and getting ready for work. She recalls her next experience, which she says was her first real contact.

It seemed her bedroom was the epicenter of the activity; she had put her kids down to bed and went up to her room. She was falling asleep when she suddenly heard a noise somewhere in her bedroom; she immediately sat up and came face to face with a non-human entity. The bed faces her closet and even though the door was shut, it looked like someone had a light on inside there. She recalled that what struck her was not so much the light or the situation, but more the sense of peace she felt. She said:

"I looked into his eyes and there was such a sense of tranquility. I knew in that moment that I would be safe no matter what. After looking into the entity's eyes, I remember getting up out of the bed and going with them, although I do not know where. It was like I walked into a dream... from there on it gets really fuzzy."

The next morning, when Connie woke up, she had a massive headache and stayed in bed most of the day. She hopped into the shower around 1:30 in the afternoon and there she noticed in the mirror a small triangular scar on her lower back. When she first noticed it, she thought maybe it was an irritation spot, as it seemed red and fresh. She remembered her dream last night; at least that was how it felt...like a vivid, surreal dream.

After a couple of days, her strange spot began to fade, although the triangle shape could still be seen lightly. With the fading of the spot went the "dream" she had. Soon Connie was back to her normal routine, although fatigue became an issue. It seemed that every night, Connie was active in her sleep and she would always wake up more tired the next morning, although she never remembered her dreams. She began resorting to power naps in the middle of the day.

One night, on the way home from dropping off one of her kids at a friend's for a sleepover, she was driving down a back road. She was always a very conscious driver; she liked to be extremely aware. She was not alone on the road that night; there was another car behind her, so when she looked back in her rearview mirror she was not surprised to see a couple of white lights in the distance. However, half way down the stretch of road, she looked into the driver's side mirror and was more than a little alarmed when she saw two sets of lights coming at her car. The lights continued to come at her and then began to flash like a strobe. This reminded her of the first time she saw flashing lights while picking up her clothes in her bedroom. Connie pulled over. She explained that it sounded like thunder as the lights zoomed by about forty feet above her car and she watched as these bright flashing lights made a quick right turn and seemed to hover for a second or two before zooming off down the road.

Since that time, Connie says it has become a regular occurrence although it seems to have no rhyme or reason. She said it happens both during the day and night, and that she feels like she is being followed. I explained to her that I did not know a cure for UFO abduction, but that I could refer her to a local ufology group. She did not want to go to anyone else; she felt as if she could trust me and that all she needed was someone to understand her situation. I asked her if she ever had the triangular mark checked; she said she had and the doctor explained that it looked almost like she had gotten a puncture wound years ago and that it had healed. He could not believe that it had happened and healed in less than a month.

Although I know she thought she was being followed, I asked her to keep track of her experiences over the next month to see if maybe there was a method or pattern to the sightings when she was in the car that she just was not seeing yet. She agreed to do so. I also asked her to keep a log of her headaches, which she said had gotten increasingly worse over the past few months. I thought that perhaps it was due to the stress in her relationship and experiences. Sometimes it is easier to see things when the issues are written down on paper and get a better perspective than in the moment.

I did see the scar on her lower back; it was very faint, although one could make out the outline. When I touched it, it felt hard...as if the whole thing was made of scar tissue rather than skin. From touch alone I could see how the doctor would conclude that it must have been a puncture wound. I attempted to take a photo of it, but unfortunately the lighting was not right for the picture to come out clear and the scar was too pale. Connie and I booked another day in the next month to get together and talk.

The following appointment was indeed a revelation. Connie said her experiences were getting more intense and the more she wrote in her journal, the more she remembered about her experiences.

One afternoon she was driving on the highway headed to Londonderry, New Hampshire, to visit some friends when she saw a deer on the side of the road. Immediately a panic seized her and she ended up having to get off the next exit. She sat parked in a fast food restaurant, her heart beat a mile a minute. Connie had never been prone to panic attacks before. As she sat in the car with her head laid back on the headrest, she closed her eyes. Visions and memories flowed through her mind....

She saw tall, thin humanoid beings and she saw herself laying on a table. She was in the dark except for a single light that these beings shined upon her. The visions were so intense she could feel the rubber type substance that the table was made of. She recalled lying on the table on her belly; her hands gripped the edge of the table as a fierce looking piece of equipment was brought over. With it, the entity took a skin sample from her lower back. Instead of pain, she actually felt a little bit of pleasure out of it. It was as though someone had pushed the backwards button in her brain making things that should hurt feel as though it was the best thing that ever happened to her. Next, she was flipped over and what she recalled next was tremendous — the non-human being placed his hand over her abdomen and she heard in her mind, "No life." That was true; she was no longer able to have kids and her last pregnancy was particularly dangerous. That was the last thing she recalled from the original abduction.

I could fill page after page with her experiences. I continue to see her every now and again, and she still keeps her abductee status to herself. Although her husband has become more open to her experiences since our meetings began, she will never tell him everything.

What I found particularly compelling were the physical symptoms and sudden phobias such as deer, for instance. This woman was never afraid of deer, a fact both her husband and family friends will attest to. She had been and still is a huge animal lover. Connie keeps a healthy diet with regular exercise and she is used to being on the road a lot as she shuttles her kids from one place to another. She had never experienced such fatigue prior to her contact. When I asked her to record her migraines, she did and we did find those to be caused by stress.

Connie is constantly aware of her health and continues to maintain herself spiritually and physically. She believes that the people she made contact with were not harmful in any way; in fact, she felt they were here to help us. I did suggest a therapist that I knew worked with a few abductees. When I explained to her that there was no judgment, she seemed to relax more. I gave her the number and as far as I know, she has been seeing the same therapist since. Connie had been offered the chance to do regressive hypnosis, but she decided against it. She feels that when she is ready to know, these entities will show her.

Signs and Symptoms of
Alien Contact/Abductions

Here are just some of the signs that an abductee might encounter. I am not claiming all abductees will experience these symptoms before or after contact, but these are the most commonly reported.

† Lost time or black outs (actions or experiences are not recalled right before and during abduction)

† Strange marks on body (odd irritation markings such as in a triangular pattern, scoop like markings on the body, laser like markings typically in geometric patterns and unexplained objects imbedded in the back of the neck, and head particularly in the nasal cavity)

† Unexplained medical issues (sinus, sudden headaches, sudden nose bleeds, and sudden back and neck issues)

† Insomnia (sudden loss of sleeping patterns and afraid to fall asleep)

† Ringing in ears (many abductees claim to hear a ringing in the ears right before and after being abducted)

† Increased dreams (dreams focused always around flying or floating in the air and through windows and doors)

† Flashbacks (some individuals experience flashbacks of their abduction that shows glimpses but not usually in full detail. Unless while under hypnosis, most abductees can then describe the full detail account of the abduction)

† Cosmic Awareness (sudden knowledge of the stars and planets in the universe, which the individual had no prior knowledge before)

† Sexual/Relationship issues (sudden withdrawal from family and friends and even sexual encounters with a spouse becomes more difficult)

† Implants (small microchips found in sinus cavity, neck, or even inside the brain, which can't be explained how or why the object got inside the individual. Some claim this microchip is in fact a tracking device that helps the aliens to keep tabs on the abductees.)

Section Three:
BOOGEYMAN
AROUND THE WORLD

Chapter Six:

THE FLESH AND BONE
BOOGEYMAN

> **NOTE:** This chapter is not for the faint of heart.
> It covers gruesome crimes from those who were
> once considered a real live boogeyman in our society.

I have covered most of the crimes in detail, but did leave some of the more disturbing bits out; in the back of the book is a list of crime websites that will give the full story of each murderer and the information that I did not include. During my lifetime, I have personally been face-to-face with many men and women who once were — *and are* — considered "The Boogeyman." I will never forget the look of no remorse on some of their faces for the horrific crimes they committed. How did I come face-to-face with such monsters? As I stated earlier in this book, for many years I served my community as a Corrections Officer for a State Prison in New Hampshire that only held male inmates. (I'm no longer doing that because I'm following my passion for the paranormal full time.) As a result, I know firsthand what it is like to be around the most dangerous criminals our society has to offer. What it is like when those large iron prison doors close behind you? ... *You enter a world that is no longer ours, but the Boogeyman's.*

ALBERT FISH

> "Going to the electric chair will be the supreme thrill of my life."
>
> ~ Fish's last words before being executed

Aptly titled "The Boogeyman" or "The Brooklyn Vampire," Albert Fish was a horror unleashed among the innocent. This sick and twisted soul committed multiple horrific murders during his reign of terror in the Roaring Twenties. Today he is a legend among serial killer enthusiasts and has been featured as one of the ten most famous serial killers of all time, but what caused his compulsion to kill? In order to find out, we need to take a close look at his childhood and teenage experiences.

Albert Fish was born in Washington D.C. in the year 1870. At the age of five, his father passed away and his mother, it seems, was primarily out of the picture. So Alfred was sentenced to life in the orphanage. St. John's took care of Alfred until he was eight years old, but even before then they noticed his odd behavior. The staff at this institution would whip children even when on their best behavior; it seemed that Alfred did not mind the whippings half so much as the other children. In fact, it may have been safe to say the whippings encouraged some of his negative behavior. Later this pattern would reappear in his life. Let us move forward now, out of the orphanage.

Albert became a repairperson in his adulthood, working for money around the local towns. He always kept to himself, but when in conversation with others he was the epitome of polite company. In 1898, Albert married, settling down into a seemingly normal life. I believe Albert loved this woman to the best of his ability. During the marriage, six children were born. This was a calm period and Albert Fish's life seemed fulfilling and worthwhile — until the year 1917, when Albert the man became Albert Fish...*the monster*.

Although Albert was committed to his wife, it seemed that she was not as loyal. She fell in love with a man who was boarding with the family. Albert tried to provide for his children the best

The electric chair that ended Albert Fish's life at Sing Sing Prison. *Courtesy of Wikipedia.*

Albert Fish's mugshot, circa 1903. *Courtesy of www.fhj.nl.*

Courtesy NYS Department of Correctional Services

he could, but the extra income from the room rental helped the family immensely. One day in 1917, Albert's wife ran away with her lover, leaving Albert to face parenthood — and all the responsibilities that go along with it — on his own, Albert's life fell to ruin, and there was only one person to blame. Was that the breaking point that turned him into a monster, or was "the monster" hiding all those years deep inside him, just waiting for that opportunity to surface?

It was not soon after that forms of bizarre and sexual acts were happing at the Fish home. Albert would force his young children to whip him in the behind with a handmade paddle that had nails sticking out of it. Sometimes the neighborhood children were forced to take part in this action. Pain was Albert's sexual pleasure in life, on himself...*and on children*. He would place cotton balls that were soaked in alcohol up his own rectum and then light the cotton balls on fire. He would burn different parts of his body with hot irons and hot pokers, and place needles down into his own groin area for sexual arousal. There were many sick and twisted actions Albert inflicted upon himself; these were just a few. Albert also tortured, molested, murdered, and ate the flesh of children over a span of twenty years. It is said the victim total was around four hundred children, but it is uncertain if there could more victims that have not been found yet.

Authorities had no clues to the disappearances of the children — not until 1928 when an eight-year-old girl went missing. Albert saw an ad in the local newspaper about a young man willing to do odd jobs. The next day he contacted the young man named Edward and wanted to hire him for his farm. When the two met, it was at Edward's home where his parents lived. The intention was to torture and murder...until Albert saw Edward's little sister Gracie. Plans now changed. Albert had to have this little girl!

That night Albert stopped by Edward's home and asked if Gracie would like to go to his niece's birthday party at his sister's house. Gracie's parents were not sure at first; they knew nothing about this stranger, but Albert was an old looking man and seemed rather nice with good intentions. There was no birthday party, but there was, deep in a wooded area, an old abandoned house called the "Wisteria Cottage." Albert told Gracie to play in the yard while he tidied up a few things before she came into the house. He undressed and called for Gracie to come upstairs. She followed the voice until she saw Albert standing in the room naked — she screamed.

Meanwhile, the time was getting late and Gracie's parents were very worried. When the next morning came and Gracie didn't come home, the parents went down to the police station to get help. They detailed what Albert Fish looked liked and the police realized that the description matched those in several other kidnapping reports. Police tracked the old man down at an old apartment building, where he was a tenant, and arrested him. It was none other than Albert Fish himself and, while being questioned, Albert gave a full accounting about his last kidnapping victim who was a young girl by the name of Gracie. When the police heard the details of Albert's latest crime, it took a lot of restraint for the officers not to throw up in the nearby trashcan. Gracie's body was in pieces and had been thrown over a stonewall near the abandoned house; there was also the meat cleaver Albert had used. The crime scene was a gruesome one and Gracie's poor parents had to hear in full detail what the police had found during Albert's trial for murder. It did not take the jury long to decide that Albert was a murderer and found him guilty.

The sentence for Albert's actions would be death by the electric chair at the Sing Sing Prison. On January 16, 1936, the electric chair took Albert's life forever. His remains were buried on the grounds of the Sing Sing Prison.

ED GEIN

Edward Theodore Gein was born August 27, 1906, in the town of Plainfield, Wisconsin. Edward and his older brother Henry were raised by unstable parents. Their father was a raging alcoholic with a violent temper and was never able to keep any type of employment. Their mother, on the other hand, worked at a local grocery store to keep food on the table for her children, but even she was verbally abusive. She was obsessed with making her two sons sit down and listen to her recite passages from the bible on death, murder, and retribution. Painful remarks about how her sons would grow up and be just like their father were always coming out of her mouth. Having friends were not allowed for the young boys, even when they hit a mature age in life. Henry was not agreeing with this at all and soon started to rebel against his mother and her views of the world.

In 1940, their father died of a massive heart attack, bringing his abuse to an end. Edward decided to take on some odd jobs to help his mother pay the bills; he helped the neighbors with painting or small repairs with the home and, on occasion, he would even babysit for them. While he enjoyed the presence of children, Edward never touched any of them in any kind of odd manner. It was as if these children understood him on a level that no adult could, especially his mother. Years passed at the Gein farmstead and both sons were adults now and still taking care of their mother. Henry distanced himself more and more away from his mother. He believed that Edward was being brainwashed by her, but could not make Edward see just how toxic this was.

On May 16, 1944, a suspicious brush fire broke out close to the Gein's family farm. Each brother went in opposite directions to try to contain the fire from spreading, but after the fire was finally out, there was no sign of Henry anywhere. Edward told the local police that his brother went suddenly missing after the incident with the brush fire, but when the police searched the grounds, there was Henry's burnt body laying on a piece of ground that had not burned. As the police looked closer at Henry's body, it showed signs of bruises on his forehead. Even with the odd evidence, the police decided to call the death "accidental" and no further investigation was done.

On December 29, 1945, Edward's mother died by a stroke at home. Edward was devastated by the death and boarded up all the rooms that his mother had used while alive, such as her bedroom and the living room. His living quarters consisted of one small room that was next to the kitchen. His world now contained an obsession with reading everything on death and dissecting human bodies. During the late night hours between the years of 1947 and 1954, Edward would visit a few local cemeteries and dig up the remains of bodies; some of those poor souls had only recently been buried.

In November 1957, a local hardware store owner named Bernice Worden strangely disappeared while running her store that day. Police had an idea just who might have been behind this kidnapping — an eyewitness had seen Edward going into the local hardware store that afternoon. When the police arrived at the Gein farm, a wide search of the property was conducted and some gruesome evidence would soon be found. During their search, the police came upon an old wooden shed; inside the shed, hanging upside down from a rope, was Worden's decapitated body. As the search continued inside the home of Edward Gein, there was more horror awaiting them. This is what the police found:

† Human skulls, which had been placed on the bedposts

† Human skullcaps, which seemed to be used as soup bowls

† Several shrunken heads

† Upholstered chair made from human skin

† A vest, which was made from a woman's torso

† Pair of socks, which were made from human skin

† Window shades pull that was made from a pair of human lips

† Several human noses in a canister

† Different parts of human organs stored in the refrigerator

Ed Gein's gravestone... Over time people have chipped pieces away to save as serial killer memorabilia. *Courtesy of Wikipedia.*

Now this list is just part of the human items that the police had found in the home. It seems that after Edward's mother had passed away, he became obsessed with the thought of becoming a woman and making a human skin suit was the only way he could accomplish that feeling.

During the court trial, it was determined that Edward would not stand fit for any form of trial and he was sent to Central State Hospital (now called the Dodge Correctional Institution) in Waupon before being moved to Mendota State Hospital in Madison. In 1968, Edward Gein was found guilty of first-degree murder, but due to being legally insane, was sentenced to spend the rest of his life at Mendota. On July 26, 1986, Edward passed away in the Goodland Hall from heart failure after a long battle with cancer.

If anyone is interested in seeing Edwards's gravestone, it is displayed at the Waushara County Museum (seems when Edward's headstone was at Plainfield Cemetery, someone had stolen it).

PEDRO ALONSO LOPEZ

"If you release me from prison, I will kill again."

~ Pedro Lopez,
speaking at his sentencing

During his reign of terror, the local villagers and newspapers dubbed Pedro Lopez "The Monster of the Andes" for his horrific crimes. He reportedly killed over 350 children. The son of a prostitute, Pedro was born in Tolima, Columbia, in 1949, the seventh child out of thirteen. He lived in an environment surrounded by poverty and violence, and all the children slept on a big bed behind a drawn curtain while his mother did her business with men.

At the age of eight years old, Pedro began to have sexual thoughts; he turned to one of his younger sisters to appease his curiosity and desires. While he was attempting to fondle her, his mother walked into the room — and she decided that the best cure for this behavior was to banish him from the home. Even though Pedro had committed such a despicable act against his sister, he was still a naïve little boy.

However, he was not on the streets long when an older man approached him. The man offered him a warm place to live and hot food to eat. Pedro was not about to say no, so when the man led him to an abandoned building, with the trust of a child Pedro followed him inside. There Pedro got his first glimpse of hell; the older man took advantage of the little boy, stealing his humanity and his innocence. After the incident, poor Pedro was dumped back onto the streets. Now knowing the dangerous environment in which he lived, he decided to roam the streets only at night while searching for food.

Pedro decided to leave Tolima and head for a town called Bogota. There, while Pedro was begging on the streets, an American couple found him and decided to enroll him in a school for orphans. He stayed at the orphanage for a few years; twelve was another turning point for him — and another hard lesson.

Pedro suffered yet another horrible atrocity; one of the male teachers at the school cornered Pedro and raped him repeatedly. Immediately following this incident, the streets became his life again and crime became his mainstay for survival. In 1969, Pedro was arrested for car theft; the judge sentenced him to prison.

Luck was never on his side. Pedro was only in prison just a few days when four inmates decided to gang rape him — and from that day on, Pedro swore no one would ever touch him again. The need to kill consumed him and, over the next several weeks, he took his revenge on each of the inmates who had raped him, taking each one out with a handmade knife. The authorities ruled the circumstances as self-defense and only gave Pedro two more years added onto his sentence. Pedro handled those extra years with a lot of satisfaction. However, the need to kill — the impulse that had been aroused while in prison — did not go away.

Wanting a chance to start over, Pedro moved to Peru upon his release from prison in 1978. Local Indian girls started to disappear, but it was not until a kidnap attempt gone awry that the locals knew what was going on. Pedro got caught red-handed attempting to grab a young girl. The local Indians did not want to settle for government justice and decided to take matters into their own hands. They tortured Pedro for hours and finally when they felt they were through with him they buried him in the ground up to his neck and left him there to die.

At some point, a missionary group came upon Pedro and helped the "poor" man out from his hole in the ground. After the authorities heard about the matter, they made the decision to send Pedro back to Ecuador, but shortly afterwards children in Ecuador started to disappear. In 1980, a flood washed out a lot of Pedro's killing grounds, including his dumping site. The bodies of several children were soon discovered as the cleansing waters washed away the dirt that Pedro had placed so carefully on top of them. Although the police knew that missing children had been reported, it wasn't an uncommon occurrence for children to run away, but when they found the grave, authorities finally realized that what happened to these kids was more despicable than even they believed and that there may be a serial killer on the loose. They then went back and looked at other missing children cases to see if there were any other suspicious disappearances.

One day, a mother was with her twelve-year-old daughter at the local market. As they perused the marketplace, an unknown man came up beside them. He casually grabbed the daughter's hand and attempted to pull her away. At the top of her lungs, she screamed and Pedro tried to run, but a local merchant caught him. As Pedro sat in the interrogation room, it seemed that he had lost his senses. He would just ramble on about nothing, but the police believed that it was one of two things: either he was scared or he just was not willing to talk and decided to evade the questions by rambling.

In order for the police to convict him, they needed a confession — they needed inarguable proof that he committed the crime and that could only come from him. Finally, the police decided to take some subversive tactics. They used Detective Pastor Gonzales to gain Lopez's trust and have the killer confide in him. The only way to do that was to have Gonzales pose as an inmate in the cell next to Lopez. Here is what Gonzales told journalist Ron Laytner, who interviewed Lopez, of the experience:

> "For 27 days I hardly slept, afraid I'd be strangled in my sleep. But I tricked Lopez into confessing by pretending I was a rapist too. He boasted to me of murder after murder in Ecuador, Columbia, and Peru. It was beyond my wildest nightmares. He told me everything."

After almost a month, the police had the confession they needed, as Pedro had confided in Gonzales vivid, graphic details of the murders. It seemed as though he had kept count of each individual child or person, their hometown, and even some of their names. In all, the total count was 110 in Ecuador, over a hundred in Colombia, and another one hundred in Peru. He explained how each girl was brought to their prepared grave, which sometimes contained bodies of other children.

Pedro went on with his story of how he killed the children; sometimes he would just strangle them and other times he would rape them first. However, he never killed them at night, for he enjoyed watching the essence of their life fade from their eyes as they died. The horror of the story continued: after the death of each child, Pedro would have gruesome tea parties with their bodies! Not sure to believe such a story, the police convinced Pedro to show them the graves of his victims. He agreed, and while most of the graves seemed to be washed away from the flood, some evidence of the other graves still existed. Pedro was finally brought to justice and sentenced to life in prison; his face had no remorse for his actions.

"I look into her eyes and see a certain light, a spark, suddenly go out. Only those who kill know what I mean. The moment of death is enthralling and exciting. Someday, when I am released, I will feel that moment again. I will be happy to kill again. It is my mission."

~ Pedro Alonso Lopez,
being interviewed by Laytner

Pedro spent the next twenty years in the women's wing of Penal Garcia de Moreno in Quito. He was the only prisoner on the wing; every day and night he was watched by a nervous three-man crew of prison guards. Pedro spent most of his twenty years worrying about whether or not he would be transferred to Colombia where he would be forced to face the firing squad as Colombia had a death sentence and Ecuador did not.

In 1999, Pedro Alonso Lopez was released from his confinement in solitary cell 29. He was then cuffed and placed into a police van. Accompanied by two other cars to protect the mass murderer from one of the family members of the 350 girls he had killed, Pedro was dropped off at the Colombian border; officials said that they deported him because he had no visa to stay in the country. They left him with a pair of shoes, a bottle of water, a few Colombian pesos, and a small package of food. This is what two of the prison officials had to say about Lopez's release:

"Yes it does sound strange, but that is our law. The law of no executions or sentences longer than 20 years was passed over 100 years ago to protect presidents of Ecuador from being killed following revolutions and military coups. In the past they had been executed in horrific ways like being pulled apart by four horses. The law seemed humane."

~ Prisons Minister Pablo Faguero

"God save the children. He is unreformed and totally remorseless."

~ Victor Lascaño,
Governor of Ambato Jail

Since that time police in all three countries keep a steady lookout for Pedro Alonso Lopez — they carry pictures of him at all times. Telephones at radio and television stations still ring all the time, reporting sightings of the "Monster of the Andes." Lopez was last seen somewhere in the mountains between Colombia and Ecuador.

PETER KÜRTEN

"Tell me, after my head has been chopped off, will I still be able to hear; at least for a moment the sound of my own blood gushing from the stump of my neck? That would be the pleasure to end all pleasures."

~ Last words spoken before being executed

Here is one of Germany's worst serial killers, who earned the title of "The Vampire of Düsseldorf." Peter Kürten came from a large family, the third eldest of eleven children. When he was born May 26, 1883, little did his mother know the monster she had brought into this world. Peter's years living at home were particularly traumatic, as he watched his father physically abuse his mother and sisters. More than that, though, his father also raped his mother and forced incestuous sex on his younger sisters.

"The whole family suffered through his drinking, for when he was in drink, my father was terrible. I, being the eldest, had to suffer most. As you may well imagine, we suffered terrible poverty, all because the wages went on drink. We all lived in one room and you will appreciate what affect that had on me sexually."

~ Peter Kürten at his trial, April 1931

At the age of nine, Peter began a friendship with the dogcatcher who lived in the same building. This man was as much a part of Peter's twisted upbringing as his father. This man introduced the idea of torture and warped sexuality. A normal child would be disgusted by the acts that Peter witnessed, but for Peter it was the opportunity of a lifetime, even at the young age of nine. He soon formed an incredibly strong bond with the dogcatcher and they were together as often as possible. I think it would be safe to say that this man was Peter's mentor.

Peter, however, was not an introvert and did in fact have friends, but soon the behavior that he expressed only with the dogcatcher began to overflow into his other relationships. One day, while

Peter Kürten's mugshot from the early 1930s. *Courtesy of Wikipedia.*

playing on a raft in the Rhine with a couple of school friends, Peter pushed one of the children off the boat and proceeded to drown him. When the other friend jumped in to save his classmate, Peter maneuvered him under the raft, keeping him there until the child also died from drowning. There was no evidence at the time to prove his actions were true and the authorities did not look any further into his confession.

In 1894, the Kürten family decided to move out of Mülheim am Rhein and settle down in Düsseldorf. Peter started to steal from local businesses and homes, running away from his own home often. He served his first prison sentence at the age of sixteen; it would be the first of twenty-seven sentences he would receive over the next twenty-four years. When his prison sentence ended in 1899, Peter refused to go back home or onto the streets, so he moved in with a masochistic prostitute twice his age. There his education was completed and what was once a fascination with animal torture turned into an obsession with humans.

Peter served his more lengthy stays in prison with bitterness, but he also realized a benefit to it. Fueled by sadistic fantasies, he would break minor rules in the prison just to be put into solitary confinement, which seemed the perfect environment to play out his perverted scenarios. Soon after his release from one of his many prison stays, Peter committed his first attack on a girl during sex. It is believed that she got away as a body was never found and that she kept silent instead of bringing charges against her attacker. With each stay in prison, Peter became increasingly resentful of society and saw his sentences as an injustice. Soon his mind went from simple sadistic pleasure and death to revenge upon a society that he believed persecuted him unjustly.

Peter's first provable murder came in 1913 during a house robbery. While the family slept peacefully inside, Peter crept into the home, where he came across a young girl in one of the bedrooms. He could not resist the opportunity and strangled her to death. He was caught by the authorities not long after and was sentenced to eight years in prison. Released in 1921, Peter decided to move to Altenburg, where he met a woman and got married. Peter, though, could not ignore the call of Düsseldorf for long. He returned there four years later in 1925... *That's when his rampage really began.*

On February 8, 1929, Peter assaulted a woman and then proceeded to molest and murder an eight-year-old girl. On February 13, he murdered a mechanic, stabbing the man repeatedly over twenty times in all. He took a brief respite, but during a three-day spree from August 21st to August 24th, he killed six people: three at separate times on the 21st; two sisters, ages 14 and 5, on the 23rd; and then stabbing another woman on the 24th. It seemed as though that he was trying to make up for lost time. However, as the body count rose, the "Vampire of Düsseldorf" left no clues and the police were stumped.

In September, Peter raped and brutally beat a young servant girl with a hammer. With each murder, it seemed Peter became more violent and more brutal. On November 7, he once more murdered, this time a five-year-old child by strangling her with his hands and then repeatedly stabbing her thirty-six times with a pair of scissors. As the next year rolled around, it seemed the murders had stopped, but then in May, Peter kidnapped a woman, brought her to his cellar, and raped her. He then brought her to the local woods, but instead of killing her, he let her go. Peter did not think the woman would remember where he lived; however he was very wrong and soon Peter was brought up on charges of rape. Still no one had made the connection between Kürten and the serial killer that oppressed the people of Düsseldorf.

Peter's wife, Frau Kürten, was the most perplexing part of the puzzle. He at one point confessed all to her, telling her the he was the "Vampire of Düsseldorf" and that she could gain a reward just for telling the police about him. He explained every murder in detail and asked her to tell the police, as he wanted nothing more than for her to live the rest of her life comfortably. When she first found out about his crimes, she insisted that they both commit suicide, but immediately Peter negated the idea. He explains:

> "Of course, it wasn't easy for me to convince her that this ought not to be considered as treason, but that, on the contrary, she was doing a good deed to humanity as well as to justice. It was not until late in the evening that she promised to carry out my request, and also that she would not commit suicide. It was 11 o'clock when we separated. Back in my lodging, I went to bed and fell asleep at once."

Even though he was a sadist, his admiration for his wife was easy to see. Here is what Peter had to say:

> "My relations with my wife were always good. I did not love her in the sensual way, but because of my admiration for her fine character."

On May 24, 1930, Peter's wife went to the police and confessed all that Peter had told her. She told them that she planned to meet her husband at St. Rochas Church at 3 o'clock that afternoon. By the time Frau Kürten arrived, officers already surrounded the place with revolvers drawn and at the ready. When Peter arrived, he made no fuss about being arrested, simply smiling as though he welcomed his fate. The rampage of murder and rape was over. Peter was finally caught. During his interrogation with the police, he confessed to seventy-nine offenses. When the trial started in April of 1931, Peter pleaded not guilty and then later decided to officially plead guilty. The judge sentenced Peter to death by the guillotine. After the execution, Peter's head was mummified and sent to scientists to be examined for irregularities in the brain. Today his head is on display at the Ripley's Believe it or Not Museum in Wisconsin Dells.

SWEENEY TODD

> "The church I was christened at burnt down the day after. My mother and father are dead, and the nurse who helped my birth hung herself, the doctor cut his own throat."
>
> ~ Part of his testimony during his trial

I have done much research on this very popular case. There are those who claim Sweeney was in fact a real person and those few who still say he was a fictional character. I will let you, the readers, make their own conclusion about this case.

Sweeney Todd was known throughout London as "The English Boogeyman" or "The Demon Barber." During the eighteenth century, poverty swept over London and most sanitary conditions for living were worse than ever. Some individuals started to die due to the raw sewage overflowing the streets, which caused diseases to spread widely. Streets became full of thieves and beggars; this was the surroundings of Sweeney Todd's birth in 1748. He was the only child of alcoholic parents. At a young age, Sweeney became fascinated with visiting the museum, which is now the famous "Tower of London." Hours would be spent on observing the torture devices and reading the stories behind them. When he was around the age of twelve, during a cold winter night, Sweeney's parents decided to travel outside and head to the local gin house for more liquor. That night would be the last time he saw his parents again. Soon after Sweeney became a ward of the state and later he was placed in the custody of a local cutler who worked in a manufacturing company that sharpened knives and razors.

At the age of fourteen, Sweeney was arrested for petty larceny, which landed him five years in Newgate Prison (known today as the Criminal Courts building). This prison held children of all ages and adults both male and female. While serving his sentence, Sweeney became a soap boy for the prison barber. He learned how to use a razor, shave, and tricks on pickpocketing while at the same time giving someone a shave.

When Sweeney turned eighteen, he was released from prison and immediately started his barber business. One day while shaving a rather dunk individual who seemed to run his mouth a little too much, the customer let it slip out about a young woman he was sleeping with. Sweeney knew of this woman, for he was living with her at the time. Those words would be the poor man's last ones — Sweeney cut him from ear to ear with his razor. The local newspapers were all over the murder, and it was now time for Sweeney to leave his woman and the town behind him.

In 1785, Sweeney bought himself a small barbershop near Temple Bar. Inside this barbershop, there stood in the middle of the floor one lonely barber chair. Sweeney had made a trap door underneath where the barber chair stood; when the lever was pulled, the chair would recline and the body would go tumbling down onto the basement floor.

Sweeny Todd's barber shop was next to a church (the skinny building on the right side of picture).

It is said that one point Sweeney took in young apprentice boys to follow his style of being a murderous barber. One young boy was drove to insanity after knowing the secrets of Sweeney's business. However, I have not come to any solid evidence of such a case. The streets of London ran with rumors of a mad barber and whispers of murder on everyone's lips. Sweeney had his shop right next to a church called St. Dunstan's and underneath this church was old crypts and tunnels that led under the city streets. It was the perfect place to hide the bodies of his customers — and he did just that.

No one knows for sure just when Sweeney met a woman named Ms. Lovett (her real first name is not given in any written account of history). It is said she was a rather homely woman who ran a bakery next to Sweeney's barber shop. There are no written accounts of anyone seeing the two out together in public, but it is written that Sweeney had long curly red hair and was always rude. With many murders, the crypts where the bodies were being kept seemed to begin to overflow and Sweeney needed another way to dispose of the bodies. Ms. Lovett had the perfect idea for solving her beloved's issue...dispose of the bodies through her meat pies.

Down in the bakery's basement was a false wall, which Sweeney had built, that led under the old church's crypts. There each murdered body would have their clothes removed, limbs severed off, and the skin on the body would be removed. After, each body had all its organs removed, was ground up, and all meat removed from the bones. Sweeney then packed up all the meat, which would be given to Ms. Lovett for her meat pies. What was left of the victims' remains were scattered all around the underground catacombs, such as the bones, heads, and other parts, which were not usable for the bakery's pies. Around the year 1924, Ms. Lovett hired a young woman and a young man who became the pie makers. (It is not known if the pie makers knew the source of the meat). Apparently these meat pies were becoming rather popular, as everyone loved the secret ingredients Ms. Lovett added in her pie making.

Meanwhile, those attending Sunday Mass at St. Dunstan's Church started to smell something awful...it only continued to get worse as time went on. At one point, the smell became so bad, the women would use scented handkerchiefs. Yet, the smell still worsened and the local priest was worried his parish would become sick due to the foul smell. He contacted the local health department and local constable to investigate what the smell could be from. During the first investigation down into the crypts, nothing was found. The smell was awful...yet the cause was not found. During the constable's investigation, he heard rumors of a local barber who murders his clients — clients would enter the shop, but no one ever came back out. Soon the constable became convinced that Sweeney was involved with the smell at the church, so he decided to have the barbershop under close watch.

A decision was made to travel back down under the church and investigate more of the crypts — and what they found would burn in their memories forever. As one of the crypt doors was opened, the men saw piles of bodies on top of each other almost reaching the ceiling. Body parts such as heads, pieces of flesh, and skeletons filled the crypt. The source of the smell had now been found. The constable noticed a pair of bloody footprints leading in a different direction...a direction that led to Ms. Lovett's bakery.

As the constable entered the bakery, he loudly announced the arrest of Ms. Lovett and the charges. When the customers found out just what type of meat was being use in the pies, the mob grew larger and wanted to hang Ms. Lovett from a lamppost. Instead of allowing the crowd to have her, the constable took her away and placed her in Newgate Prison until the trial, but there was one more loose end to clear up and that was Sweeney Todd. Not long after, Sweeney was picked up and was also placed in prison to await trial. While Ms. Lovett was being questioned by the authorities, she had no issue with giving away all of Sweeney's plans.

In December 1801, inside the prison walls, Ms. Lovett took her own life by poisoning herself. Now it was just Sweeney to stand trial for the murders, but no bodies could be identified because of being so decayed. Nevertheless, the authorities did have all the

Fleet Street was the Demon Barber's hunting grounds, circa 1890. *Courtesy of Wikipedia.*

Fleet Street, circa 2005. *Courtesy of Skyring.*

clothes and property of 160 people, which had been found during a search of Ms. Lovett's home and Sweeney's shop. When the jury was excused from the case to deliberate, they returned within five minutes with a guilty verdict. Sweeney was then sentenced to death by hanging. On January 25th, Sweeney was led to the gallows. Thousands of people came out to the prison to watch the mad barber be hanged. The court decided to donate the body of Sweeney to the local barber-surgeons. Now it was his turn to end up just like his victims...lying in a pile of flesh and bones on the floor.

Chapter Seven:
BOOGEYMAN IN THE MOVIES

> "One, two…Freddy's coming for you!
> Three, four…Better lock your door!
> Five, six…Grab your crucifix!
> Seven, eight…Better stay up late!
> Nine, ten…Never sleep again!"
> ~ from "Nightmare on Elm St."

Like most individuals, I am a huge fan of horror movies and especially all of the Wes Craven and John Carpenter movies I grew up watching — and still watch even to this day. Nevertheless, I have to ask, what is it that we love so much about these types of movies? Getting scared? Maybe it is seeing a reflection of our worst fears and knowing that it is not real? Are we thinking that just maybe these Boogeyman types could be real?

In the state of Rhode Island in the 1800s, there was a real man named Charles who later was nicknamed "Fingernail Freddie." He became terribly burned and horribly disfigured while trying to save his family from a house fire, which was set by local kids who used to sneak on his property and let out his farm animals from the enclosure. Charles had enough with these local kids and decided to teach them a lesson. He filled a rifle with salt pellets and the next time those kids came onto his property, he fired and hit a few of the kids with the salt pellets. With stinging wounds, the kids ran off.

The next day, the kids decided to go further and make Charles pay for what he had done to them the day before. The idea of setting his small cabin on fire was the perfect plan for their revenge, but not for Charles's family who were inside the cabin at the time. His family was burned to death while alive and, now with his overgrown fingernails, he seeks revenge on the locals for the deaths of his family. There are rumors that he dwells deep in the woods in the town of Cumberland, just waiting for those who dare to enter and for those to never be seen again. (The full story of Fingernail Freddie is in my book *Rhode Island's Spooky Ghosts and Creepy Legends*).

I have to wonder how twisted some of these horror writers must be. What makes them write these horrible, blood-curdling tales? What — or who — is their inspiration? Could it be perhaps a local legend or an article of a crime reported from the newspapers or seen on the local news channel. These main characters are from some of my favorite movies and are the epitome of the boogeyman. They scare us, excite us, and sometimes they even make us think, but more than anything...they resonate with us and bring out our deepest primal fears.

MICHAEL MYERS

"Halloween"

It is a quiet Halloween night in the small town of Haddonfield, Illinois. The year is 1963 and a young six-year-old boy by the name of Michael Myers is home with his seventeen-year-old sister who is watching him while their parents are out for a night on the town. Out of nowhere, Michael, looking as though he was in a trance-like state, approaches the kitchen and slowly opens the drawer where the cutting knives are kept. He stops for a second and then pulls out a large knife and quietly heads upstairs where his older sister is talking on the phone with a friend. Michael did not seem to notice that he was still wearing his Halloween costume of a clown and has his mask over his face. He enters his sister's room and violently begins stabbing her repeatedly. The parents finally pull into the driveway, smiling and rejuvenated after their night out. What they see next is burned into their memory forever. They go upstairs to check on their kids and find their daughter laying in a pool of blood on her bedroom floor. Michael is just standing there, looking not affected by his actions or his sister's death. Michael's parents did not know what to do with him after that, so he was sent off to an asylum called Smith's Grove.

There he meets Dr. Sam Loomis who is assigned to him as a pediatric psychologist. With Michael safely locked away, life seems to go back to normal. The days wax and wane in the town of Haddonfield; eight years pass before anyone sees or thinks of Michael Myers again, although, amongst children, his name is still whispered as legend. At the asylum, Michael sits in his cell as if waiting for something or someone. By this time, the doctor is convinced that Michael is more than just insane; he believes Michael is evil. Year after year, Michael would just sit in his room and not move. Dr. Loomis was nervous about allowing Michael to be transported to court, but the judge demanded that Michael be charged as an adult for the gruesome murder of his sister. All hell breaks loose during the transport and Michael escapes. Stealing one of the institution's vehicles, he speeds off to his childhood hometown. Did I mention it is Halloween again?

Dr. Loomis has a good idea of where Michael is headed and travels to the same town looking for him. Meanwhile, a young woman named Laurie is looking out the window during class at school and notices a strange figure of a man wearing a white mask standing there watching her before then disappearing. On her way home from school, she sees the same strange figure behind a bush, but as she walks closer to see, no one is there.

By now its nightfall and Laurie is getting ready to meet her friend Annie who is babysitting a little girl down the street. The phone rings and it is the neighbor across the street from where Annie is babysitting. They are going out to a Halloween party and really need someone to watch their young son for a few hours. Laurie, being nice, agrees and calls Annie back to tell her she will not be able to make it because she was asked to babysit. She then heads out the door...the masked man all but forgotten.

Annie calls Laurie at the house where she is now babysitting and asks if she will watch the little girl while she goes and picks up her boyfriend. All is fine and Annie sends the little girl across the street to where Laurie is babysitting. As Laurie is closing the door, the little boy catches sight of a "Boogeyman" behind Annie and sees a large knife. He screams and tells Laurie what he saw; she blows him off thinking it is just the fears of kids at Halloween and sends the children to bed.

Some of Annie's friends stop by the house where she is babysitting; the door is unlocked and they go into the home. The young couple looks around and figured Annie went off to get her boyfriend, so they decide to go upstairs and fool around a little. Michael is in the house...a fact the young couple soon finds out firsthand.

Some time goes by and Laurie is getting worried about Annie, knowing she should have been back a while ago. Laurie keeps calling the phone, but then gets a strange phone call, which is not Annie at all, but from Michael himself. Laurie keeps the door open as she walks across the street to see what is going on. She goes into the home that Annie was staying at and discovers all three of her friends covered in blood and murdered. Laurie screams and runs out of the house to go back to where she is babysitting across the street. Michael pursues her and drags Laurie into the house; the young woman looks around in terror, trying to find a weapon. She reaches for the nearest object and, finding a knitting needle, she quickly turns and stabs Michael in the neck and runs upstairs to get the children out of the house.

As the children run screaming out of the house, Dr. Loomis sees them and knows what is going on. He heads towards the house and enters. Laurie is fighting for her life, as Michael has grabbed her by the neck and is attempting to strangle her. Just then, the doctor runs into the bedroom and commands Michael to let the young woman go. He does and then the doctor shoots Michael six times, which makes him fall off the two-story balcony. Right before the story ends, the doctor looks over the balcony and sees that Michael's body is gone.

If ever a boogeyman story freaked me out, this would be the one to do it. Intrusive and violating, the Michael Myers character is the epitome of a person's worst fears; someone with great strength, stealth, and supposed immortality. He cannot be killed, but he loves to kill and he can gain access to homes without making a sound or drawing attention. No matter how fast you run, his slow and steady gait will always be faster than yours....

CANDYMAN

"Candyman"

During the 1800s a young man, who was the son of a slave, became rich by an idea of a shoe-making machine (which later the written script was changed to him being a portrait painter) and he soon fell in love with a local plantation owner's daughter. With clandestine meetings and midnight kisses, she soon became pregnant with his child. The daughter's father became filled with anger. He could not believe that his daughter was carrying a baby...that she was of such loose morals and would disgrace the family name by sleeping with someone beneath her station. He gathered all the other local men to find the young man. He was soon found and chased through a meadow until he was caught by the men. The locals began to cut off his right hand and smeared his body with honey, then allowed the bees to come and sting him to death. After the young man had died a slow painful death, the men burned his body.

The scene opens right into two women who seem to be graduate students; both are doing some research about local urban legends for their thesis. The two women decided to interview some local inner city students about legends and overhear a legend about a man named Candyman. Intrigued, the women decided to dig deeper into the story. The students also talked about the way to summon this nefarious character; in a very close variation of the Bloody Mary myth, look into a mirror and say "Candyman" five times and he will come for you.

Helen, the story's heroine, decided to follow some more leads to a certain housing project that is overrun by a local gang. Here she discovers an abandoned apartment, where supposedly the Candyman had murdered a woman years ago. After investigating the murdered victim's apartment, Helen decides to knock on the apartment next door. A young black woman opens the door and is not very happy to have visitors. Neither is her dog. Helen talks with the woman for a short time in her apartment and then heads back home. While parking her vehicle in the parking garage of her apartment, Helen encounters the Candyman and suddenly faints. Next thing Helen knows she is lying on the floor in the apartment of the woman she had just interviewed hours ago. All covered in blood, Helen hears a woman screaming and struggles to get up off the floor. Someone had beheaded the woman's dog and kidnapped her baby. Helen stood standing there is shock, trying to figure out what was going on. Nevertheless, before Helen could think, the young woman lunged at her with a knife. Helen gets the knife away from the other woman and cuts her; as that happened the police broke the door down.

At the police station, Helen tries to convince the police as to what is really going on. No one wants to believe her, though, and she is charged with attempted murder and placed into a mental institution for evaluation. Meanwhile, the Candyman visits Helen's thesis partner and kills her.

By this time, Helen is beyond freaking out, as the Candyman visits her while she is in restraints in an isolated room at the hospital. When Helen is calmed down, she is brought into one of the doctor's office to talk with the psychologist. Helen is again trying to explain what is going on when suddenly her restraints, which are tied to the chair, are cut loose by an unseen force. Candyman is now standing behind the doctor who is sitting down behind his desk. As Candyman tries to sway Helen to his side, the doctor is seen with blood coming from his mouth. Candyman's hook is deep inside the doctor's back and he dies sitting in his chair. Helen runs away and sneaks out of the hospital and heads back to the housing projects. She notices that the residences have placed a large pile of wood in the yard for a party that night that is to include a bonfire.

Candyman has the woman's baby and tries to bribe Helen by giving her the baby. Only he tricks her and now the baby is inside the pile of wood for that night's bonfire. Helen climbs into the pile of wood and sees the baby all the way at the bottom. Just when Helen grabs the baby and heads back out, Candyman appears and tries to kill her. By this time, the residents have gathered outside to light the bonfire. Flames suddenly take over the wood and Helen is trying to escape the grip of the Candyman. At last she does and, as she is making her way out of the fire, she is now burning alive. Helen crawls out onto the ground and makes her way to the crowd, but only has enough strength to hand the baby back to its mother. Then Helen dies.

A twisted love story, but a love story nonetheless. I love this take on the myth and could watch the Candyman saga repeatedly. He is a scary boogeyman and, while he seems to have lost all of his humanity, as the series continues, you see his character evolve. From the beginning, there is pity for him and fear for the victim. However, by the end of the series it is almost as though you are rooting for him! He does not come out of closets, but much like Bloody Mary, he is a child's worst fear. This movie is a great example of portals, as the Candyman uses the mirror as a gateway to our physical realm and can only be sent back to the ether by fire.

FREDDIE KRUEGER

"Nightmare on Elm Street"

It is the year 1940, around the Christmas holiday, and a young nun who worked at a psychiatric hospital called Westin Hills was soon faced with a terrifying event that would change her life forever. While doing rounds, the nun became accidentally locked inside a criminally insane ward known as "the tower." Here the worst one hundred of the insane individuals were kept. Her "will" would soon become broken, as she was repeatedly raped and tortured over and over. Days later, her bloody body was discovered and not long after the rape, she finds out that she is pregnant. Nine months later, Frederick Charles Krueger was born.

After a long labor, which ended in a breech birth, the child was placed in a foster home to be adopted. Frederick eventually ended up in the home of an abusive, alcoholic man who tormented little Freddie. Reaching adulthood, Freddie settled down and married. Not too long after, he became the father of a beautiful baby girl.

After Freddie murdered his adoptive father, the family moved into the home that he grew up in at 1428 Elm Street. Suddenly children started to go missing and their bodies found dead days later. At some point unknown, Freddie's wife stumbles upon a secret room in the basement where she finds strange torture devices and different types of clawed gloves. Newspaper clippings of the murders were sprawled out everywhere inside the room, and now his wife knew the truth. This would lead to Freddie strangling her to death in the backyard after his wife comes out of the bulkhead to the basement and begins interrogating him about the room. His daughter was in the backyard as well and looked on in horror as she watched the spark go out of her mother's eyes.

Deep inside the town's local power plant where Freddie had worked at, he would bring the local children into the boiler room and kill them there with his razor claw glove. The total was around twenty local children. Soon the police were on Freddie's trail and arrested him in 1966 for the murders. In 1968, the judge had signed the search warrant, but he signed it while under the influence of alcohol and signed his name in the wrong place. All charges were dropped because of this and Freddie was again free to murder. We come to find out that his young daughter was placed in foster care for a short time before being adopted by a stable, loving and normal family. We also discover that Freddie's real mother (the young nun who was raped) hanged herself in the now abandoned Westin Hills — in the same room that was once called "the tower" — after she read about Freddie's release.

Everyone knew Freddie was being released and there was nothing they could do to stop him from coming back. However, there was something they could do to stop him from killing ever again...or so they thought. They decided to take justice into their own hands and get revenge for all of the children that Freddie took away from the community. They all headed to the power plant knowing Freddie would not be able to resist going back to his old stomping grounds. They poured gasoline on the boiler and around the rest of the room. They then just sat back and waited for Freddie's return — they did not have to wait very long.

When Freddie finally arrived, he went right down to the boiler room, ready to relive his glory days and start his reign of terror again. The parents lit the gasoline on fire, trapping Freddie in the room with the boiler. As the flames consumed him, three demons that found the most evil of souls had a deal for Freddie: they would bestow upon him the gift of immortality for the souls of innocent children; in return Freddie would be given the power to turn dreams into reality and would be able to murder as many children as he wished. The deal was sealed with Freddie's death of burning alive. The burned remains were hidden away by the children's parents at an auto salvage yard and placed inside the trunk of an old red Cadillac. Hidden away forever...or so the parents of Elm Street thought.

To erase the brutal terror, which had shocked the neighborhood, one of the families decided to move into the old Kruger house and bury the past. However, as the surviving children grew into teenagers, something started to go very wrong. In 1981, local teenagers started dying off in unexplained ways while sleeping. With each soul taken, Freddie was once again becoming powerful. He battles with one teenage girl who is eventually able to overcome him and kick his butt! She escapes Elm Street, but so does Freddie. Knowing that people are on to his game, he leaves in search of another town — one that does not know his name — so that he can be free to kill forever.

Somehow, Freddie ends up meeting his real daughter and tries to convert her to his way of life. She rejects him and the fight begins. His daughter knew the only way to defeat her father was to bring him out of the dreams and into her world. She did just that and stabbed Freddie in the stomach with his own claw glove. She then quickly shoved a homemade pipe bomb into his chest and killed him. The three demons that had given Freddie his powers vanished and left his body forever.

If there ever was a movie character I would want to sit down and have coffee with, I think Freddie would be it. He is scary, campy, and his sense of humor is morbid. Freddie is a typical boogeyman figure and, for young children, it can be a horribly scary experience watching a film like this. However, as adults, Freddie is a comical villain. The back story of Freddie Krueger is far too real; child killings happen every day, so this resonates with us as parental figures. It's a parent's worst fear...being unable to protect our children and that even in dreams our children might not be safe.

AFTERWORD

Writing parts of this book unlocked memories of my own childhood that I thought I had forgotten…memories I forced myself to forget until now. Little did I realize that by experiencing these traumatic events, it would someday lead me to a career involving the darker side of the paranormal (becoming a demonologist). Today, I travel all across the United States and beyond to help individual people or families suffering from every type of haunting; sometimes these families even believe they are truly dealing with the Boogeyman.

I was once asked why I write these books and there are two reasons. The first is simple, I love it. The second is, for the knowledge. I have always been the type that looked for answers. The one thing I want anyone who reads my books to feel is that they have learned something new or useful. I am arming you with the ammunition, so that in case you ever come into a similar situation, you are already fully prepared. Knowledge is power — remember that!

While doing research for this book, there seemed to be so many different types of theories behind the truth and legend of the Boogeyman. By covering spirits, nightmares, myths, legends, alien encounters, and even real life serial killers, I hope you have found answers to those puzzling questions. Is the Boogeyman real or not? I believe he is, whether it is in the form of a spirit, a serial killer, or a movie monster. The Boogeyman lives in the deepest darkest corners of our minds and the nightmarish reality of our dreams. Remember...that shadow lurking in the corner of the room might not be a shadow at all, but the Boogeyman himself.

Be Safe.

Katie Boyd, Demonologist/
Occult Sciences Expert

BIBLIOGRAPHY

Bird, Chris. "Planetary Grid." *New Age Journal*, May 1975.

Childress, David Hatcher. *Anti-Gravity and the World Grid*. Kempton, Illinois: Adventures Unlimited Press, 1987.

McHargue, Georgess. *The Impossible People*. New York, New York: Holt, Rinehart and Winston, 1972.

Morfill, William Richard, and Robert Henry Charles. *The Book of the Secrets of Enoch*. Filiquarian Publishing, 1896.

OTHER RESOURCES

Here are some great sites worth checking out.

Paranormal websites:
www.katieboyd.net
www.beckahthepsychic.com
www.planetparanormal.com
www.unexplained-mysteries.com
www.ghostvillage.com
www.trueghosttales.com
www.paranormalencyclopedia.com

Sleep Disorder and Medical websites:
www.stanfordhospital.org
www.sleepcenters.org
www.narcolepsynetwork.org
www.mentalhelp.net
www.epilepsy.com

Horror movie websites:
www.allhorrormovies.com
www.theofficialjohncarpenter.com
www.wescraven.com
www.holloweenmovies.com
www.freddykrueger.com
www.horror-web.com
www.deathndementia.com
www.fearnet.com

UFO websites:
www.ufomag.com
www.legendarytimes.com
www.mufon.com
www.unknowncountry.com
www.cufos.org

Real life boogeyman websites:
www.serialkillercalendar.com
www.allserialkillers.com
www.albertfishfilm.com
www.trutv.com
www.knowledgeoflondon.com

More Interesting Websites

www.samuraidave.wordpress.com: Has an awesome page on the Namahage.

www.archangels-and-angels.com: This is a good place to start learning about the different angelic correspondences and how to work with them.

www.sofritoforyoursoul.com: It has great information about the El Cuco.

www.sacred-texts.com: It offers a wide assortment of spiritual texts both ancient and out-of-print.